The woman whose spirit is being crushed and whose life is endangered by domestic violence needs straight answers—not unrealistic expectations or clichéd, stereotypical platitudes. In this book, she will get straight answers, clear scriptural direction, and some tough challenges from one who has been there but is there no longer.

CHRISTIANS
&
DOMESTIC VIOLENCE

Jocelyn Andersen

ONE WAY CAFÉ PRESS
Auburndale, Florida, USA

Woman Submit! Christians & Domestic Violence
Copyright © 2007 Jocelyn Andersen
Cover Design: J. Andersen and Van-garde Imagery, Inc.
Book Design : J. Andersen
Book Layout: Van-garde Imagery, Inc.

Published by One Way Café Press
Auburndale, Florida 33823
ISBN-13: 978-0-9794293-0-9
ISBN-10: 0-9794293-0-7

The artwork of Kathryn Hartman Isler is used by permission.
The Poem *"The House on Taft Street"* by Kathryn Isler is used
by permission.

*Over a period of nine years, the author experienced abuse
and domestic violence through two abusive marriages. For
simplicity's sake, in this book, the marriages are treated as
one composite marriage.*

One Way Café Press provides timely and relevant resources
for Christian growth and victorious Christian living www.One
WayCafePress.com

Biblical references are from the King James Version

Printed in the United States of America

Books By Jocelyn Andersen

Redemption: Bible Prophecy Simplified

125 Years of Bible Version Debate: Why?

My Denomination Does Not Promote New Age
Spirituality Through Spiritual Formation!

Woman Submit! Christians & Domestic Violence

Acknowledgements

The subject of domestic violence is not a subject I would normally choose to immerse myself in. God knows it is only by His grace that I was able to complete this work at all. I confess I set it down and allowed it to collect dust far too often while burying myself in other projects.

Butch, you deserve a medal for putting up with being married to a writer. I love you.

Terry James, thank you for your prayers and encouragement concerning this book and also for your practical advice and efforts on my behalf—an unpublished author, and when I first contacted you with my seemingly unending stream of writing questions—a total stranger. I pray I never give you cause to regret your kindness and support.

Thank you, Joyce Hart, for your brutal honesty about my writing not being very good when you read your first sample of it. You have to know that sent me scrambling back to my shelf of writing handbooks. I hope it has improved since then.

Thank you, Kathy Isler, for your generous permission in allowing me to tell your story through your artwork. I know many hearts will be touched by it, as mine was, and I pray they will be inspired to extend their compassion towards the battered and abused women within their spheres of influence.

There are so many who have inspired and encouraged me in so many ways to finish this work, I cannot possibly name you all in the space permitted. But you know who you are, and I thank you from the bottom of my heart.

Thanks, Mom, for always keeping your door open. I love you.

Contents

Foreword

Jocelyn Andersen experienced domestic violence first hand and has survived to write about it. However, what she writes in these pages is more than just a testimony, it is an appeal. Andersen strongly appeals to any woman who is experiencing domestic violence at the hands of her husband to leave. Her appeal is specifically targeted towards Christian women because Christian women are more apt to stay in a potentially deadly situation due to what they've been taught in regards to the interpretive meanings of the scripture passages that deal with submissive roles in marriage and limited exceptions for divorce.

It is sobering to realize that many of the clergy in today's church believe and teach that a woman must, at all costs, not divorce her husband, even if she is constantly living under threat of death in her marital home. Andersen bravely and boldly challenges doctrinal teachings that discourage women from leaving husbands who are abusing them.

Andersen writes in conversational tone. So, reading her book is like hearing her voice. She writes in such a way that you can hear her talking to you. You can hear her inflections through the pages. Moreover, it's a quick read. I read most of it in one setting.

Although Andersen and I don't completely see eye to eye when it comes to her theological viewpoints regarding Adam and Eve, her book is in no way heretical. Just to clarify, when Anderson says "lives are more important than theology" she's not talking about the theology of salvation (for those of us who are Christians should be willing to give our lives, if need be, for the sake of the gospel of Jesus Christ), but she is instead talking about the theology of marriage and divorce. And when a woman is faced with making a decision between getting away from an abusive husband or staying in a life-threatening domestic situation, I agree with Andersen; to live is more important. What earthly good are we if we are dead or if things are so bad at home that we wish we were?

I believe that any abused woman who reads this book will be encouraged to get help. To be quite honest, I believe this book could save lives.

Praise God for Jocelyn Andersen and the work she has done in her effort to help women through the trials of domestic violence and abuse.

~Elreta Dodds
Author of, *Is God a Chauvinist?*

From the Author

Although there are different scenarios within the arena of spousal abuse and domestic violence, this book presents just one—primarily my own personal experience, observations, and insights which I have found (through surveys, conversations and correspondences with many abused and/or battered women) to be quite typical.

The reader will find no advice in this book on recognizing the signs of a potential abuser, reaching safety, or navigating the legal system. Nor is there advice on step-by-step healing *after* experiencing domestic violence. There are already books and resources that cover these things in great detail. It is not my intention to try and duplicate or replace other good works dealing with the subject of domestic violence, but rather to complement them.

I am also aware that women are not the only ones who suffer from abuse and violence at the hands of spouses. Although this book is written primarily as a resource for battered women (97-99% of battered spouses are women), most of the insights and advice given to battered/abused wives in this book can be applied to husbands as well, should the situation be reversed.

About the Artwork

As already stated, there are many different scenarios within the arena of domestic violence. The artwork in this book is the work of Kathryn Hartman Isler. Kathy was a victim, but is now a survivor, of 21 years of spousal abuse. Her story, told through her drawings, is different from mine in many ways and the abuse she experienced much more severe. But I believe her experience is representative of the combined experiences of many battered women and serves not only as a comparative parallel to my own story, but, in many instances, contrasts it as well—adding critical balance to this work.

More of Kathy's artwork can be seen on the following websites: http://www.ladywind.com/whatwords.html http://www.intimateemotions.com/KathrynHart manSets.html

A Broken Life

Because the depression I suffered was
so severe, I put down my art many
years ago. But . . . I realized that I
must do something or lose my sanity . . . so it was that my art was born
anew. I found that I could draw what
I could not express verbally. . . .

Kathy Hartman Isler

Introduction

Fear, desperation, pain, humiliation, and confusion
are constant companions to all women who experience abuse of any sort at the hands of their husbands.
But the evangelical Christian woman finds herself
faced with the unique burden of also needing to know
the specific will of God concerning her situation.

I call this a unique *burden*, because assimilating all
the conflicting information she receives from books,
well-intentioned Christian friends, family members
and spiritual leaders can leave her head spinning—
and her ego spiraling . . . in precisely the wrong direction. To make matters worse, the counsel she receives often ranges from disappointing at best to life-
threatening at worst.

The practice of hiding, ignoring and even perpetuating the emotional and physical abuse of women is
still rampant within evangelical Christian fellow-
ships, and as slow as our legal systems have been in
dealing with violence against women by their husbands, the church has been even slower.

Abuse among Christians often creates a cruel catch-
22, as many evangelicals view recommending separation or divorce as unscriptural, but then view the
battered/abused woman with contempt for staying in
the situation and tolerating the abuse.

Victims quickly pick up on this hypocritical attitude and either leave the church altogether—or begin hiding the abuse. Either way, they are forfeiting the spiritual guidance and emotional support they so desperately need.

The Christian woman whose spirit is being crushed and whose life is endangered by domestic violence needs straight answers—not unrealistic expectations or clichéd, stereotypical platitudes. In this book she will get straight answers, clear scriptural direction and some tough challenges from one who has been there, but is there no longer.

Ministers, friends and family of the abused will find the book informative, useful and challenging as well.

Spousal abuse and domestic violence was not introduced into my life until I reached my late thirties, so I understand both sides of the issue very well. Prior to the abuse, no one could have convinced me that my attitude toward battered and abused women was both casual and condescending, or that I would ever tolerate it myself—yet it was, and I did.

As both a minister and a woman who has experienced abuse, I feel I can contribute a unique, personal perspective to the small but growing data base of books concerned with the issue of domestic violence.

My own experience, together with research and the feedback I have received from many other battered women, has convinced me that, even in these "enlightened" times we live in, the battered/abused woman is still very much alone and confused in her struggle.

It is my prayer that this book will provide answers, bring hope, and prove to be of practical value to both the battered/abused woman and to those she is most likely to turn to for help.

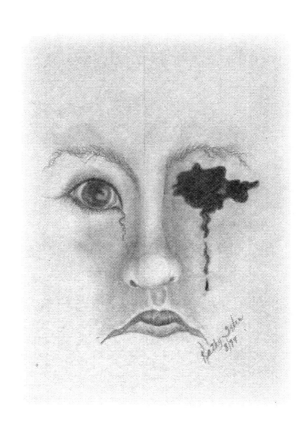

By the English common law, her husband was her lord and master. He had the custody of her person, and of her minor children. He could 'punish her with a stick no bigger than his thumb,' and she could not complain against him.

"Massachusetts in the Woman Suffrage Movement"
Harriet H. Robinson, 1881

Canadian novelist Margaret Atwood
once asked a male friend why men
feel threatened by women. He replied: "They are afraid women will
laugh at them." She then asked
a group of women why they felt
threatened by men. They answered:
"We're afraid of being killed."

1

I Should Be Dead . . .
But I'm Not!

I shall not die, but live, and declare the works of the Lord. . . .

The Holy Bible

My pastors and I had made the difficult decision not to hide the abuse from our church family any longer.

As a member of the Praise Team, I was accustomed to standing before the congregation, but this particular evening the bruises on my face made the public appearance a bit more difficult. Due to the unusual absence of my husband, the person responsible for the bruises and an *associate pastor* of our church, it was imperative that the issue be dealt with as quickly, delicately, and honestly as possible.

He was evading arrest. This was the second time in six months he had tried to kill me.

~~~

21

Friday, 8:30 a.m., August 29, 2003
In my distress, I called upon the Lord . . . .

"Jesus won't help you!"

With those words ringing in my ears, John brought his loafer-encased foot crashing down onto my face. Then, as suddenly as the violence started — it stopped.

I sent up a silent prayer of thanks, saying, "*Yes you did, because everything stopped.*" It had not yet occurred to me that I was lying on my back, staring at the ceiling, in a different part of the room, and in a completely different position than I had been in just moments (or so I thought) before.

John was standing over me, pacing back and forth and ranting about letting me live—*this time*. It wasn't until he stopped, looked down at me, and said, "Oh my God, *look at you*," that I realized the violence must have continued even after I cried out to Jesus for help. It also began to dawn on me that I could not raise myself up from the floor. I was not in any pain. I simply could not get up.

After John lifted me off the floor, I knew he must have injured me very badly. Besides not being able to focus my eyes clearly, close my mouth all the way, or sit or stand without assistance, I was afraid I was going into shock. Although it was August and very hot outside, I was freezing—shivering violently.

I asked him if he would take me to the emergency room. He said, "No, you'll call the police." When I asked if I could call someone else to take me to the emergency room, he said, "No, either God will take care of you or he won't."

It was obvious he was afraid he had fatally injured me, and I could see that my repeated requests for help were beginning to agitate him. I knew I had said all I could safely get away with, so from that point on, I asked for help only from God. I consigned myself to His care and began praying for rescue.

There was a telephone on the nightstand just next to the bed I was lying on, but I was too injured to reach for it. Unable to do the slightest thing for myself, a portion of the sermon our assistant pastor had preached just two days previously kept running and re-running through my mind. "The devil," he said, "comes to steal, to kill and to destroy, but *I have come . . .*" Those words were like a lifeline to me. I repeated them over and over to myself and said to the Lord, "You came, Jesus. You *came. . . .*"

But the circumstances seemed hopeless. I was injured, isolated, and completely helpless. I was at the mercy of a man who had just tried to kill me and was steadfastly refusing to allow me to receive help of any kind. He was more willing to allow me to die than to face possible arrest and conviction for assaulting me.

John's emotions appeared to be on a frightening roller coaster. His behavior was erratic and unpredictable. One moment he would appear to be calm and treat me very gently, the next, for no apparent reason, he would begin raging again—particularly against women he felt wanted to *rule over men*. At one point he spoke about having to leave the house and told me he would be forced to tie me up while he was gone. I absolutely knew if he ever did that he would feel he had no choice but to go ahead and finish me off. My position was precarious at best. Whenever I was forced to speak to him or answer his questions, I chose my words very carefully. I knew only the Holy Spirit could help me navigate the situation and keep me alive until help came.

It concerned me that I did not have a definite sense of the Lord's presence. I remember asking, *"God, where are you?"* He answered my question with a question of his own, **"Do you feel this peace?"**

Yes I did. And I knew that peace only came from one source—God. It was good to know I was not alone.

I had not looked in the mirror yet, so I did not know I had what the emergency room physician would later describe as "raccoon eyes," a discoloration caused by bleeding from the eyes. I had not yet seen that my right jaw was grotesquely swollen, though it concerned me greatly that I could not close my mouth completely—I could not bring my teeth together. I felt certain I had a broken jaw. I was experiencing severe dizziness and equilibrium problems. I could not sit or stand without assistance; walking was completely out of the question. I was very nauseous. Each time John lifted me to a sitting position, I began retching violently. If he let go of me, I collapsed like a rag doll. I was having severe problems with my vision; I could not focus my eyes clearly on anything. And whenever I moved, even slightly, the vertical hold on the room would spin out of control. Within a short while, I also realized blood was seeping from both ears. The emergency room physician said some of my symptoms corresponded with those of a skull fracture, but besides a mild headache, the only real source of pain I experienced came from my right hand and arm which were fairly useless. That was my condition for about 20 hours.

Sometime during the early hours of the next morning I woke up and realized I felt different. I felt *better*.

I thought, "*I think I can sit up*," and I sat up. I thought, "I think I can *stand up*," and I stood up. I thought, "I think I can *walk*." And I walked!

I knew that a supernatural healing from God had taken place while I slept.

This was an exciting development. The first thing that occurred to me, of course, was not to tell John. I reasoned that if he thought I was still helpless, he might relax his guard and I could get away from him. But instructions from the Holy Spirit came quickly and clearly—I was not to try and deceive him. It did not seem at all logical, but I knew I had heard from God. So, when daylight came, I confided to him that I had been able to get up by myself during the night. His answer was chilling. He said, "I know—*I was awake.*

 My imprisonment continued, but in spite of my desperate circumstances, the peace of God guarded my heart. I was in a deep sleep most of the time. I awoke at some point during the second morning and found myself alone; of course, I headed straight for the telephone. *But it wasn't there.* John had removed all the phones from the house.

This was a *big* problem, because even though I could walk and the visual disturbances I had been experiencing were now gone, my balance was still extremely poor. I was still very weak, and I was too slow and unsteady on my feet to attempt leaving the house with no guarantee that anyone would be nearby to help.

We had a large fenced front yard that, in my condition, looked as large as a football field. I knew it would take me quite a while just to make it to the street (climbing the fence into the neighbor's yard was not a physical possibility), and if John came home before I cleared the yard, it would take no effort at all for him to drag me back inside. If that happened, I knew that I would not survive the consequences of trying to escape. I was confident the Spirit of the Lord was leading me not to try just yet.

When John returned, I asked, "Am I a prisoner?" He said, "No." I was nervous about questioning him, but felt a boldness to go on. "Then why are all the phones gone?" He said he had removed them so I could not call the police. I promised him, before God, that if he would return the phones I would not call the police—*and he did!* Then he left again.

But now I had another problem. I had just made a vow before God that I would not call the police. I stared at the phone and mentally worked through my options—breaking my vow was not one of them.

I did not know how much time I had before John returned, and most people I knew lived at least twenty miles away. Simple things overwhelmed me. I could not remember telephone numbers, and John had taken my cell phone that had my frequently called numbers programmed in it. The phone book wasn't any help, because (besides my mother and my pastor) I could not think of anyone to call. *I could not remember who I knew.*

I picked up the cordless phone, looked at it, thought about it—then carefully replaced it.

I knew I was having a difficult time thinking clearly, but, again, I was confident God was leading. John returned after being gone only a short while and made a point of looking to see if the phone had been moved. It had not. I had returned it exactly as he left it. Then, after a few hours, he left again.

This time, with no hesitation, I picked up the phone and quickly dialed my pastor's cell phone number. God's timing is always perfect—my pastor and his wife "just happened" to be in my neighborhood—only blocks from my home. Within minutes I was safely on my way to the emergency room where X-rays and an MRI confirmed what I already knew: nothing was broken, and there was no internal bleeding—because God had already healed me of the most serious of the injuries that had been inflicted on me *32 hours* earlier.

There is not a doubt in my mind that I should not be alive today to tell this story. I am convinced that, had it not been for the immediate and supernatural intervention of a great and mighty God, my life and death would already be a statistic.

I would either have mysteriously disappeared at the hands of my husband, or my family and friends would most certainly have found me—within a just few days, lying in my home—beaten to death. And every year on August 29th, they would celebrate a heartbreaking anniversary. For some, pilgrimages to my gravesite would be made with flowers and heavy hearts filled with remorse. Others would be tormented by memories of missed opportunities—guilt would gnaw at them for the miserable comforts they had offered in their frantic, but ineffectual, concern for my safety. They would wish with all their hearts they could take back unkind and condescending words and actions they now understood had only acted as wedges—alienating them from their beloved daughter, sister, mother or friend.

But what could they have done differently? What could my pastor, family or friends have said or done that could have helped me? What could *I have done* that could have helped me? And why couldn't I have done it sooner?

These questions must be answered. *Lives* depend on it. It is time to stop the useless rhetoric. *Why doesn't she just leave? If she stays, she deserves what she gets . . . well if I were her. . . .*

Well we're *not* her!

To my everlasting shame, there was a time in my own life when I said the same hateful things. I knew that *I* would never tolerate abuse. My attitude towards the battered woman was more condescending than compassionate. Certainly she was an object of my pity, but more so of my contempt . . . until I unwillingly joined her ranks.

Then I experienced, first-hand, the terrible dynamics that bind a wife to an abusive husband.

If this book helps shed a little light into a very dark arena from the perspective of one who has been there but is there no longer—if it can help induce compassion where formerly there was little or none—perhaps save a life and give a happy ending to someone else's story, then it will have accomplished its purpose.

In this I am reminded of the story about a small boy walking along a beach that was littered with dying starfish. It seemed thousands of them had been washed ashore, but the little boy walked patiently among them picking them up and, one by one, throwing each back into the ocean where it belonged.

A gentleman approached the boy and asked why he bothered. How in the world, the man asked, did he think he could make a difference when there were simply too many to throw them *all* back?

In reply, the boy stooped down, picked up another starfish, tossed it into the waves, and said, "It makes a difference to *this* one."

And that is all any of us can do—try and make a difference for *this* one—for the one who may be looking to *us* for help.

Being a support to a battered or abused woman is a frustrating experience at best and frightening at worst. She is often indecisive and cannot be counted on to keep her promises to get out, and stay out, of the line of fire. Her abuser holds tremendous emotional influence over her . . . and we do not. The temptation is great to throw up our hands and say, "I'm through with you! You deserve what you get! Let yourself be beaten to death if that's what you want!"

But do *not* do it.

We need to remember that we are merely inconvenienced—she is genuinely suffering and possibly in very real danger. Our friendship and support can make all the difference to an abused woman in the face of seemingly overwhelming circumstances. Our friendship and support can help make her existence a little more bearable, thereby giving her the strength she needs to make choices that, ultimately, may help to change her circumstances and possibly even save her life.

"Be careful not to get too involved. If she goes back, then you won't be so frustrated for helping her. . . ."

Anonymous Miserable Comforter, 2005

I expected to feel relief when
he left, not the pain of
abandonment that I do now. . . .

Former Battered Wife, 2006

It's hard to leave. It's terrifying
to think of . . .

Kathy Isler

2

Widowhood Descends

Bear ye one another's burdens, and so fulfill the law of Christ... rejoice with them that do rejoice, and weep with them that weep.

The Holy Bible

Few can understand why a wife would grieve the loss of a spouse who abused or battered her.

I remember how relieved I was to get away safely after that final brutal assault. But I was completely unprepared for the devastating sense of loss I experienced. My husband, who I genuinely loved, and my marriage, along with all my hopes for it, was just . . . gone.

It was sudden. It was complete. And it was irrevocable. In one fell swoop, the circumstances of my life, and how I perceived those circumstances, completely changed.

In a very real sense, widowhood had descended. And I wept . . . and almost *no one* wept with me.

Yes, it is a good thing when a battered wife is finally in a safe place. That usually only happens when she is away from her husband. But few realize she has just experienced a painful amputation. And her grief is compounded by the fact that she usually has no one who can bear this burden with her.

She is usually surrounded by those who rejoice in her loss.

For safety reasons, I had to leave my home and move in with family, and while I rejoiced in God who saved me, I bitterly grieved the loss of my husband. *But I did not dare let it show*. While I was hiding my grief, my family openly rejoiced that my marriage was over, a marriage I had tried with all my might to save, and freely vented their rage towards the one I was grieving for.

I understood their rage stemmed from their love for me (and from their fear for my life and safety). But I was suffering, and they simply could not comprehend the struggle I was having dealing with the terrible sense of loss and displacement I was experiencing. I was convinced that many of those who claimed to love me would have heaped abuse on me themselves if I had let them see even a glimmer of what I was going through.

I wanted to go home, but I had no home. I wanted to belong somewhere, but I did not belong anywhere. I wanted my husband, but I had no husband. . . .

My grief was very great; and my comforters, though they did not intend it to be so, were mostly miserable.

Thankfully, my church family handled the emotional aspect of my situation somewhat better than my biological family did. Although few of them could comprehend the depth of my loss, they at least understood that I had suffered one. Most of them were experiencing a loss of their own in connection with the situation. My husband had been a well-known and generally well-liked associate pastor of our church, and until the evening my pastor and I made the facts of our private lives public, most of our fellow church members had no idea he was also a wife-beater.

It is a credit to that small, inexperienced congregation that I did not feel compelled to completely hide my grief from them. Few of them were comfortable with bringing up the subject of my ship-wrecked marriage with me, but absolutely no one rejoiced in my loss (at least not in my presence) or rebuked me for grieving it. They truly did try to bear my burden with me, and I will forever be grateful to all of them for that.

I will never forget the first Thanksgiving after my marriage ended. Our church had a special service with guest singers and a church full of visitors, and the pastor opened the floor to anyone who had a special testimony of thanks. I had one—but did I dare share it? It was an ugly thing God had saved me from. Would I be contaminating the beautiful service we were having by bringing up such a subject? Would it be proper to inflict the memory of my "dirty laundry" on our members and visitors?

I felt the Holy Spirit wanted me to share my testimony. So I stood and declared to the glory of God how I had lived and not died. And then, still not sure if I had done the right thing, quickly sat down. I was barely seated when a note was passed to me from one of the ladies visiting our church that morning.

"Please call me . . . " it said.

It turned out she also had "dirty laundry" in her life. But she had never felt free to ask for help from her church family in bearing her burden, much less felt free to testify about how God had brought her through her troubles with domestic violence. That was the first time she had ever heard such a thing during a church service.

I have yet to share my testimony publicly and not have some woman in the gathering approach me afterwards with her own story of abuse or domestic violence.

I later confided to my pastor's wife my hesitation in bringing up such an ugly subject during a church service. Her wise words brought me great comfort. She said, "That is your testimony. You cannot hide it."

She was right. It should not be taboo to discuss such things at church. When we are with other members of the Body of Christ, we should feel free to be ourselves. Fellowshipping with other Christians should be the safest place on earth in which to be transparent. We should all be willing to help bear one another's burdens, whatever they may be. The scriptures command it.

But how can we do that if we have *no* idea what those burdens are?

Crumbling Life

Learning comes from life's
experience......sometimes the
lessons come too late.

"Society usually labels women who are victim-
ized by abusive men as fools for ever having
gotten involved with them. But the word of God
identifies the angry and abusive man as the one
who is the fool . . . "

Elreta Dodds
Is God A Chauvinist?, 2002

3

The Shame of it all

"What's wrong with you that you marry people like that?"

Emergency Room Physician —"Christian" Counselor wannabe

erhaps if we lecture the battered/abused woman enough it will shock some sense into her, and she will stop allowing herself to be assaulted. . . .

Oops, did I just say the word *assaulted* again?

Well, saying that, let me say this: *regardless* of the circumstances, no one *deserves* to be assaulted. And while we're at it, why aren't we calling a spade a spade? Why isn't assault always called assault? If a stranger is doing the attacking, it's called assault. If a spouse or parent is doing the attacking, it's called *domestic violence* or child *abuse*.

Assault is assault. So why do we tolerate semantics that soften the appearance of a crime? I am not splitting hairs here; semantics are very important. Ask any advertising agency or expert on propaganda.

In most people's opinion, assault is most definitely a crime, but in the case of domestic violence—*well . . .* the waters get a bit murky in that area, don't they?

For centuries no one wanted to get involved with other people's "family troubles." What went on between family members was their own private business. Then, when laws were finally enacted to deal with these things, the issue was approached gingerly, and the crime was watered down with soft language. However, legally, domestic violence *is* a crime. So having established that a crime has been committed, let's establish one more thing. Whether it is a stranger or a family member doing the assaulting, the one *committing the crime* is the criminal. The one doing the assaulting is in the wrong—*not the person being assaulted.*

So, why is it that the *victim* of domestic violence always feels so ashamed?

One of the worst things I have had to deal with since being assaulted is the shame I have experienced resulting from attitudes directed at me, on an ongoing basis from friends, acquaintances, family members and even total strangers. The reproach has been very difficult to deal with.

The general attitude seems to be that if I knew he was abusive (and I did), then it was my fault that I *let myself* be assaulted. Because of the prevalence of these attitudes, it was only natural that I avoided telling people what was going on during the abuse, but I was surprised to find that negative attitudes towards battered women seldom improve even after they leave the relationship.

After the experience described in chapter one and before my violent husband was arrested, I had to deal with being stalked by him, so I moved to another town (far enough away that I felt safer, but close enough to get to my business and church with only a short commute). I felt very good about the fact that my new landlady, who lived next door, kept a grandmotherly eye on me. That being the case, it was inevitable that she would notice some of the precautions I was taking in order to avoid having my location detected. So when she asked me about them, I felt very safe sharing my story with her.

As she looked through the stack of police photos I showed her, witnesses to the brutality of the assault, her response absolutely blew me away. Blaming me for the assault, the only thing she had to say about what she was seeing was, *"aren't you a better judge of men than to marry someone like that?"*

Sigh. . . .

I had heard almost the same question from an emergency room physician after the assault.

I should be accustomed to these attitudes by now, but it does not seem to work that way. I was blindsided during a telephone conversation with a family member while discussing a matter completely unrelated to my experience with domestic violence. To my utter horror, I found myself being slammed because I had previously been an abused/battered wife! This missile came out of nowhere—almost *two years* after I had left the relationship.

Even though I had ended my abusive marriage, the disdain and contempt this family member felt towards me in regards to my former situation seemed to have remained unchanged. And he had the unmitigated gall to accuse me of behaving no differently than an addict! I was so shocked and hurt by his reproach that I did not bother telling him I actually agreed with him. All the shame I had been dealing with for years came flooding back with his accusations, and instead of trying to make him understand, I quickly ended the conversation and hung up the phone.

As serious as physical injuries from the batterer can be, the emotional wounds of shame and reproach inflicted by others, especially by those who claim to love the battered or formerly battered woman, can be much worse. I have long since recovered from any physical injuries I received, and forgiven my abuser, but dealing with ongoing contempt and bias from the most unexpected sources has been very difficult.

Another occasion that stands out occurred about the time of my first wedding anniversary (after divorcing my violent spouse and marrying the wonderful man I am married to today). I was testifying to a woman I had just met about the great things God had done for me, and the story of my experience with domestic violence came out. The only response this woman had to my story was to question the wisdom of my remarriage! I have found that people feel very free to criticize the battered or formerly battered woman— whether they know her well or not.

There seem to be many who are more willing to stand in judgment of the battered woman than those who would demonstrate compassion. And because of this, I have frequently found myself shying away from sharing the domestic violence part of my testimony. When I do choose to share it, the inevitable question of, *"Had he ever been violent before?"* usually pops up. It took a while for me to realize this is really a qualifying question—a question designed to categorize me. The real questions being, "Are you a repeat case? *Did you bring it on yourself* by not leaving him for good the *first time* it happened?"

I was flabbergasted, one day, to hear myself denying that my ex-husband had ever been violent more than once. I had been asked point blank if he had, and I told a bald-faced lie. Of course I confessed the lie, and I remember telling the person I lied to,

"I don't know what made me say that!" It had been completely unpremeditated, and until that moment I had not been aware of how much the shame of it all had been affecting me. But I had obviously had come into agreement with the consensus that there was less shame involved in being assaulted once, as opposed to being assaulted repeatedly.

The shame heaped on battered women because of their implied *weakness* and *stupidity* in *allowing themselves* to be assaulted more than once eventually becomes too much for them to deal with and is a major cause of withdrawal from sources of potential protection and support. I have spoken with many battered women and have yet to find one who, due to shame, did not withdraw from the very people she should have been turning to for support—and that frequently includes, as in my case, the police.

The battered woman becomes very vulnerable to anger and bitterness, not only towards her abuser, but towards contemptuous and disdainful friends, family members and others. These very damaging emotions, along with depression, can become paralyzing making it even more difficult for her to reach out for help in any kind of proactive manner.

Even after a violent relationship has ended, friends and family often treat her as if she is completely incompetent when it comes to relationships with the opposite sex and in choosing a lifelong companion.

I remarried fairly quickly after my violent marriage ended. I did not feel I needed another husband and was not looking for one, but God, in his infinite wisdom, had other plans for me. I did not tell *anyone* in my family that I was getting married. My church family was present at our impromptu marriage ceremony, but not a single member of my immediate family was there. The reason for this was because I had regularly been told, prior to my marriage, *"Now don't you go getting married again!"*

The admonition was an absolutely humiliating epitaph to most conversations I had with many of my family members in those days. This revealed that in their opinion, unconscious though it may have been, it was in reality *my* fault I had been battered due to my own incompetent choices. My family's opinion of my decisionmaking capabilities had obviously sunk to an all time low, and I was at a complete loss as to how to deal with it.

Well, I did *go and get married again*. But I was made to feel so ashamed of this decision, even before the decision was made, that it took me a week or so to gather up enough courage to tell my family about it.

I am now married to a remarkably kind and wonderful man, and it was a painful experience to witness his being ostracized from family gatherings, because of the prevailing attitude that anyone I chose to marry might not be safe for my grandchildren to be around.

My husband was on probation with my family until it was proven to their satisfaction that he was not dangerous (even though, usually, the only person who is not safe around a wife-beater is his wife!).

Since I refused to submit to that kind of abuse and disrespect from my own family, or to subject my husband to that kind of humiliation, I was deprived of seeing a new granddaughter for several months. My sister, who was outraged at the treatment we received, could not have nailed it better when she said, "It's bad enough you had to go through what you did without everyone blaming *you* for it!"

I do not write these things as an indictment against my family. I write these things because I have come to realize that my family's response was not at all unusual with respect to the situation. It seems to be an almost universal response that the battered woman is ultimately blamed for the abuse. And even though her family and those closest to her may not consciously realize this is what they believe, they demonstrate it in many ways that hurt and humiliate one who has already endured more than her share of pain and humiliation.

And this is not simply my opinion. This opinion is reinforced by the fact that judges across this country frequently rule against battered wives in child custody proceedings and grant the batterer custody in divorce cases based on the fact that the wife tolerated being beaten in the first place! Decisions like these reflect the fact that many judges not only place the blame on the woman for the fact that she was battered, but they also feel the wife-beating criminal is the more stable and responsible parent!

To the Christian who should be strengthening the battered sister (mother, daughter or friend), who is already beaten down enough, but is instead heaping judgment, contempt and disdain upon her, let me say this, "Shame on you! Brethren, these things *ought not to be.*"

To battered and abused Christian women, who are fairly crushed by these attitudes, let me say this, "Jesus hears the cry of your hearts, and he will answer you—*without rebuke.* And *if* you will acknowledge him in all your ways, he *will* direct your paths."

Rage

The question is often asked of abused women, "*Why don't you just leave*?" **Look at RAGE.** Can you see an answer here? This is why I didn't leave for so long. I was afraid! I had *no voice*. As the years went by, he had so torn at my confidence and self-esteem, that my soul and spirit felt as if they were in **shreds**, and I was literally terrified of being on my own, of being away from the house, of being around people. I was even afraid to be "just me . . . "

And who was I anyway? I didn't know.

Kathy Isler

4

The Eve Syndrome

. . . and thy desire shall be to thy husband . . .

The Holy Bible

Why do men beat their wives?

With domestic violence against women being the leading cause of injury to women worldwide, it should surprise us that this is not the number one question being asked about the issue today. But sadly, it is not.

Although it is one of the things we *should* be asking, the number one question everywhere is, *"why doesn't she just leave?"*

I have been guilty of asking the same thing myself.

The question of why she stays has given rise to some outrageous conclusions, some of which have become deeply rooted within our culture. Some of these have gained such widespread acceptance that even well known and highly respected individuals continue to reinforce them—much to the detriment of battered women.

One very insidious and persistent myth of why she stays is that battered women thrive on the abuse and derive some sick satisfaction from it. That opinion coming from non-professionals should not really surprise us. Most of us have heard it at one time or another. Many of us have *said* it at one time or another. But I do not apologize for nearly going into shock when I heard it coming from a highly respected, well known, expert in family counseling.

Not only is this person heavily credentialed, but he is also one of the darlings of the evangelical community. He is held in such high esteem, that I was bluntly told by an experienced literary agent that no Christian publisher would touch this book if I did not exclude the things I write about him in this chapter and the next. But because of this man's widespread influence due to a prominent ministry, radio programming and best-selling books, I could not in good conscience do that.

In a 1984 broadcast of his radio program, "Focus on the Family," Dr. James Dobson told his listening audience that he had seen situations where the wife wanted to be beaten up. He hypothesized that she achieved a certain moral advantage from being hit; and that if she pushed her husband into blacking her eye, the whole world—God included—would see that she was really a martyr. He said she did this in order to feel as if she were in charge and to give herself a moral exit from the marriage, because the Bible says marriage is forever.

Granted, Dobson said these things in 1984; that's quite a while back. But research which disproved his theories had already been published before he made that statement. He said basically the same thing in his best-selling book *Love Must Be Tough*, which was first published in 1983. When the book was revised in 1996, not one word in the domestic violence section was changed. And it is that edition which is featured on the "Focus on the Family" website, touted as a best seller, and still stocked on bookstore shelves today.

In *Love Must Be Tough*, Dobson revealed his profound lack of concern for, as well as lack of insight into, the issue of domestic violence. His lack of concern is revealed by the ridiculously small number of pages he devoted to the subject (five). And his lack of insight is revealed by his setting forth as a fair example of battered women the story of a woman he believed to have provoked abuse from her poor "non-communicative" husband (who was presented as one to be pitied) in order to gain a "prize," in the form of bruises, which she could then "show off" in public.

Dobson not only does nothing in this book to help the plight of battered women, but actually makes things worse for them by propagating and reinforcing age-old prejudices and misconceptions such as the myth about women who, for whatever reason, enjoy being beaten and "bait" their good husbands until they give them what they want.

James Dobson is highly regarded among evangelicals, and has had incredible opportunities to either help or harm the cause of battered women, but in a 236 page book dealing with the subject of disrespect and abuse within marriage, he saw fit to dedicate only five pages to an issue which he acknowledged as becoming an epidemic. Of the paltry five pages he did commit to the subject, one and one-half of these were used to illustrate how one woman *baited* her husband in order to induce the battering!

The particular woman Dobson portrayed in his book may very well have had a sick motive for provoking her husband to violence, but is she a fair representation of the vast majority of the millions of women who are battered each year or of the more than one thousand, in this country alone, who die?

Dobson's analysis and general application of this sick situation has been read by evangelicals for over 20 years now and has no doubt adversely affected both their perceptions and their treatment of battered women—leaving many women without the unbiased support they desperately need from their spiritual leadership.

I am not denying that situations like those Dobson described can and do happen, but given the scope of his influence within the evangelical community, and given the limited amount of space he devoted to the issue of domestic violence in *Love Must Be Tough* (add to that his confession that he did not believe he had anything relevant to add to what had already been published on the subject), it is my opinion that battered women would have been better off altogether if had he just kept silent.

With the plight of battered women coming to public attention only sporadically, figuring out why women stay in violent/abusive situations hasn't been of paramount importance to most of us. It has only been within the past few decades that cultural concern for battered women has been exhibited in any tangible form such as shelters and more immediate consequences to wife-beaters via arrest and prosecution. However, the question does linger, and in 1979 Dr. Lenore Walker decided we needed to have a definitive answer to the question of: *Why doesn't she just leave?* She attempted to give us an answer in her book, *The Battered Woman.*

Walker hypothesized that the battered woman experiences a phenomenon called "learned helplessness" and also (among other things) an irrational belief that the abuser is omnipresent and omniscient. These beliefs, Walker claims, cause her to seek and develop survival tactics rather than escape tactics. Thus, she is prevented from leaving the relationship.

At last battered women were getting some positive attention and official recognition of their dilemma. The term "battered woman syndrome" (BWS), coined by Walker, turned out to be great news—to the relatively few women who had escaped their situations...by *murdering* their abusers. Defense attorneys were quick to jump on the bandwagon. And, today, with the majority of states allowing BWS to be introduced as evidence in murder trials, we know that Lenore Walker's theory has been accepted, by and large, with open arms.

But do we really want to give her the last word on the subject? In spite of the obvious compassion which motivated Walker to deal with the subject, and I commend her in that, has her hypothesis truly improved the lot of battered women? The evidence leans heavily to the contrary.

As more and more states are allowing BWS to be introduced as a defense in murder trials, more and more judges are requiring the women claiming this defense be *diagnosed* as having "the syndrome" by undergoing a psychological evaluation. So now, in addition to other negative stereotyping, battered women have conveniently been labeled by the legal system under the guise of "helping" them, as having a mental illness!

The woman who chooses to stay in an abusive marriage typically deals with an incredible amount of condescension from those closest to her. And the negative attitudes of those who should be a support to her can be major players in the depletion of the spiritual, physical and emotional strength she desperately needs in order to effect a change in her situation. Although Walker, to her credit, in subsequent editions of her book, stressed that BWS should not be classified as a mental illness, but rather as a subcategory of Post Traumatic Stress Disorder, the battered woman is, never the less, viewed as having a pathological condition.

I reject the idea that women stay in abusive marriages because they become mentally ill. And I am not the only formerly battered woman who feels this way about such theories. In a statement made by formerly battered and battered women, published by the National Coalition Against Domestic Violence (NCADV), the battered woman syndrome is obviously referred to when these women strenuously object to being described in clinical terms saying, "We will not be defined as having a psychological malady because we have been battered."

And if the additional labeling and stereotyping isn't bad enough, since BWS has been embraced so enthusiastically within our nation's courtrooms, another very frightening question has been raised—if a mother is diagnosed with having battered woman syndrome, is she a fit parent? This question is being considered more and more, and battered wives are finding themselves losing their children *to the batterers* in child custody proceedings.

This development is also addressed in strong language in the following statement made by the NCADV: "The Battered and Formerly Battered Women's Caucus of the National Coalition Against Domestic Violence call upon all battered woman's projects, organizations and workers to stop using clinical language and mental health/social work models in their work with battered women and children . . . while this approach may have gained respect and financial advantage for some battered women's workers, this language has done so at the cost of re-victimizing, disrespecting and demeaning battered women. It has also inadvertently aided batterers using institutional systems to persecute battered women in areas such as child custody proceedings."

I see Lenore Walker's BWS as further stereotyping an already heavily stereotyped group of women and introducing further threats into the lives of women who are already threatened to the limits of their endurance.

The temporary value of BWS to the cause of battered women is evident, with its major advantage being seen in the courtroom where a woman may have the chance of avoiding a murder conviction due to a diagnosable mental illness induced by the abuse.

The legal status of BWS in the majority of our state courtrooms sends a clear signal that our society is satisfied with the negative label bestowed upon battered women (however reluctantly) by Lenore Walker. It is also obvious that, to the satisfaction of most American judges, the question of "why she stays" has finally been answered.

It is a crying shame more people are not asking the question, "Why do men beat their wives?" But whether we like it or not, the question of why she stays will most likely continue to hold first place.

There are many pressures, such as fear, economic problems and social isolation, which are inevitably brought to bear on the battered woman who attempts to leave her abuser. Add to that the fact that the woman who does leave faces a real possibility of losing custody of her children and increases her chances of being killed by a margin of 75%, and we get a fairly good picture of why many women don't "*just leave.*"

At the time of this writing, I am corresponding with the family of a battered wife who escaped her situation but was forced to leave her young daughter behind. This mother is devastated by the loss of her daughter and at the same time terrified, with very good reason, of facing her abuser in a court battle which statistics show she has a good chance of losing.

In addition to these valid reasons for not "just leaving," the scriptures reveal another, more basic, reason why a woman may find it difficult to leave a violent marriage.

I believe the scriptures answer both questions (why she stays and why he does what he does) more than adequately. And although to some it may come as a complete surprise, psychologists are *not* the experts on the human condition—Jesus Christ our creator is.

Psychology is a human invention which largely denies the spiritual aspect of humans as well as even the existence of God, much less his active participation and interest in our everyday lives. On the other hand, doesn't it make sense that the one who did the creating in the first place would understand exactly how the creation works and why it behaves the way it does?

Genesis 3:16 has this to say about wives and husbands, *"Thy desire shall be to thy husband, and he shall rule over thee."*

This verse has been quoted for centuries to establish the irrefutable fact of God given male supremacy in marriage. Multiple millions of God-fearing men and women throughout the ages have bought into, and suffered from, the consequences of one of the most tragic misinterpretations of scripture ever. Christian men and women have accepted almost unchallenged the erroneous idea that when the serpent, Eve, and finally Adam were informed of the consequences of their sin, God slipped Adam an unexpected and undeserved bonus.

He got to be the boss!

And why would this be one of the most tragic misinterpretations of scripture ever? Because innumerable lives have been ruined, and even lost, as men and women struggle, often their entire lives, trying to make sense of a most insensible premise.

In the case of Adam and Eve, we see that one of the consequences of the couple's sin was an abusive reaction from Adam which brought a surprising response to the abuse from Eve.

When the first man rejected his wife, and betrayed her horribly, by blaming the entire debacle of their joint rebellion on her alone, the first woman was driven to hope obsessively for the transformation of her husband's character and the restoration of their relationship to their original conditions.

We see evidence of this in the fact that Eve, at the birth of her third son Seth, was still clinging desperately to the promise that a male child, descended from her, would make all things right again and restore the perfect life they had previously enjoyed (Genesis 3:15).

Eve believed God's promise, and she knew her only hope of true happiness lay in its fulfillment. So at the birth of Seth, we see her rejoicing, because God finally blessed her with another male seed (Genesis 4:25).

There is no doubt that when Cain and Abel were born, she was certain one of them was the promised one. But when Cain killed Abel, she knew she must wait for another. Unfortunately for Eve, Seth wasn't the one she had been waiting for either. It wasn't until after the birth of his son, Enos, that men finally began calling on the name of the Lord.

It is an interesting fact that Enos wasn't born until Adam was 235 years old. So if we believe the scriptures, we have to believe that after Abel died, there was not a male on the planet worshipping the Lord until after Enos was born.

My question to all this is, "What was *Adam* doing all that time?"

I believe he was working hard, trying to feed his family, just like God said he would—*by the sweat of his brow*. And while the sweat was pouring, instead of praying, Adam was bitterly complaining and lamenting his great losses. Paradise was lost, his son Abel was lost, for all practical purposes his son Cain was lost, and what was Adam left with? The *woman* God gave him. And he blamed her for everything.

We know this, because in Genesis chapter three we see Adam playing the blame game to the hilt. We see him blaming the woman for his sin, and we see him blaming God for giving him the woman in the first place. He had all his bases covered—he thought.

Scriptural evidence points to the fact that after the fall, Adam continued his plunge into a downward spiral of anger, bitterness, and self-pity which resulted in continued blame and bitterness towards God, as well as bitterness, blame and abusive behavior towards his wife.

Adam's response to the consequences he suffered for his sin is typical of the response of today's abuser. His predicament was everyone's fault but his own!

Adam simply would not face up to what he had done, nor would he take personal responsibility for his own actions and the resultant losses. And we find nowhere in scripture that he ever repented from these sinful attitudes, but we do find evidence to the contrary.

In Genesis 3:16, we see God telling the disobedient pair that, as a result of sin, Adam and Eve's godly directive to dominate the earth would be perverted, in Adam, into a dysfunctional desire to dominate his wife (*he shall rule over thee*).

I refuse to accept the traditional theological interpretation of that verse to mean that Adam was rewarded for his sin by being promoted to a higher status within his marriage.

This, therefore, is the scriptural misinterpretation which has been perpetuated for so many centuries: The Lord God was not *commanding* Adam to rule over his wife, he was simply informing them both that the easy companionship and equality they had previously enjoyed together was now a thing of the past. The two were destined *never* to enjoy it again. Sin had irrevocably altered their lives.

Sin continues to have a detrimental effect on relationships. And what we need to understand about the consequences of Adam's perversion of the original godly directive, is that environmentally as well as spiritually, it was passed on to all of his male descendants.

Here are a few statistics: Approximately 32% of women murdered each year are murdered by their husbands or male companions—most often as they are attempting to escape the violence. FBI statistics for the year 2005 show that 1005 women were murdered by a husband or intimate partner that year. These are statistics on *solved* cases only. And they are only statistics for the United States. Add world-wide statistics along with historical numbers to these, and anyone can agree that a great deal of tragedy and ruin has taken place over the centuries.

Dr. Susan Forward, in her book, *Men Who Hate Women & The Women Who Love Them*, states that a boy raised by an abusive father, " . . . can absorb his father's contempt for women very early in life."

Can anyone deny both the scriptural and the empirical evidence that Adam was very likely the world's first abusive husband, and as such would have been the first father to pass on his abusive attitudes to his sons?

But Adam was not alone in his destructive attitudes toward females. I believe that Eve, inadvertently, was just as responsible for the enduring legacy of prejudice against females we still see and experience today in virtually every culture and society on earth.

Remember, God told the couple it would be a *male* child who would defeat the serpent and restore everything back to its original perfection.

Eve had to be desperate for that boy to be born. She was most likely pregnant a good deal of the time, and multiple births would not have been unusual for her (Genesis 3:16). She only gave birth to three male children and Seth was the last of these. 105 years passed between the births of her son Seth and her grandson, Enos (with no telling how many daughters and granddaughters in between—daughters born to her and Adam and daughters born to Seth and his wife [or wives]). Her keen disappointment at the birth of each female would have been nearly impossible to hide, and it would have been very difficult for her daughters and granddaughters not to have absorbed and emulated Eve's attitude. Her example would naturally have been that it is preferable to give birth to a male as opposed to a female, and that attitude still prevails, in most cultures, to this day.

Due to the consequences of Adam's sin, the natural inclination for the males of our species is to have a strong desire to be in charge. An encouragement in this sinful tendency is the notion of male supremacy that has been reinforced theologically for centuries by male-dominated clergy. Because of this, there are men who feel they have a mandate from God to reign supreme within their homes, and some will take that mandate to an abusive, dangerous—even deadly— extreme.

Instead of detaching herself from these disrespectful attitudes and maltreatments; instead of a resultant loss of love and desire for her abusive husband on the woman's part, the natural female response often seems to be an even more intense desire for her husband's love, affection, and acceptance (*thy desire shall be to thy husband*).

She seeks to appease him and improve him so he can be transformed into the loving companion she so desperately wants and needs—and has never given up hoping he will become. She wears rose-colored glasses and is driven by a hope that has little basis in factual reality. She endures incredible amounts of emotional and physical pain, because she loves him and believes that her love, sprinkled here and there with a few ultimatums (from a safe distance when necessary), can change him into a kind considerate human being who realizes just how much he loves and needs his wife.

When a wife responds in this way to abuse (more often than not encouraged by her spiritual leadership), she is not demonstrating a pathological aberration. She is responding normally—exactly the way the Lord God predicted she would.

I have chosen to call this perfectly normal, predictable, and prophesied response... the _Eve_ Syndrome.

Resigned

"I **RESIGNED** myself to the **false** fact that I had no choice..."

Kathy Isler

The primary responsibility for a good relationship in marriage lies with the wife. If the wife is submissive to her husband, they'll have a good relationship.

Reverend Marvin De Hann
"Have You Excommunicated Your Spouse?"
Good News Broadcaster, March 1982, p. 47

The scriptures say a woman must ignore her feelings about the will of God, and do what her husband says. **She is to obey her husband as if he were God himself.**

Elizabeth Rice Handford
Me? Obey Him?, 1972

4

Church Sanctioned
Oppression

*He that dashes in pieces is come up before thy face: keep
the weapons handy, be alert, strengthen yourself, get **strong**
reinforcement!*

The Holy Bible

W hen a woman who is being battered finally
becomes desperate enough to approach her
pastor or other spiritual advisor for help,
rather than being offered any kind of proactive solution, the counsel she receives can often lead her to
take a very dangerous, passive approach to dealing
with her problem.

The passive approach centers almost completely
around the unbiblical strategy, and uncertain out-
come, of *changing her spouse* through *reacting* to his
abuse in a manner prescribed by the church.

Those who think the evangelical church has kept up
with the courts and various social agencies in encouraging and assisting battered women to participate proac-

tively in protecting themselves from violence are sorely mistaken. It was only a few years ago that I heard the following exchange on an evangelical talk radio show:

Caller: How should I respond to my husband's anger, alcoholism, adultery and *abuse*?

Host: You are a missionary in your marriage. If he is willing, you should hang in there and pray for him.

Before reeling off this traditional but very possibly dangerous piece of advice, the minister hosting the program made *no effort* whatsoever to find out the extent of the abuse this woman was experiencing or if there was the possibility of an immediate threat to her physical safety. I was left reeling from the shock of hearing this woman being dealt with in such a casual, irresponsible manner.

The caller's husband may not have been simply behaving badly. There was a very real possibility that his behavior was not only criminal but could have been life-threatening as well. Had this woman truly been a missionary, the members of her mission's board would most certainly have encouraged her to flee that particular mission field and head for safer ground immediately.

The "stay and pray" counsel may be applicable in most marital disputes, but in the case of domestic violence *it is not*. It only serves to enable the abuser to comfortably continue his sinful and *illegal* behavior while keeping his victim in harm's way. But such counsel is commonly accepted among evangelicals as the Biblical solution to domestic violence.

When a battered wife wrote James Dobson that the violence within her marriage was *escalating* in both frequency and intensity and that she feared for her life, he replied that her goal should be to *change her husband's behavior*—not to get a divorce (*Love Must Be Tough, 1996*).

He did suggest leaving as a temporary solution, but only as a way of manipulating the husband's behavior. I found it inexcusable that not one note of real concern for this woman's immediate physical safety was sounded in his response—in spite of the fact that she clearly stated she was in *fear for her life*.

Dobson counseled her to precipitate a crisis in her marriage by choosing the most absurd demand her husband made, then refusing to consent to it. This was not only absurd advice in a domestic violence situation, but life-threateningly dangerous as well, and very telling of the fact that, in spite of over 1000 deaths per year due to wife-beating, the wife beater is not generally viewed as a real threat to his wife's life or safety.

The option of legal recourse, such as arrest and prosecution for her husband's criminal behavior, was never mentioned, and no spiritual or emotional remedies, such as church discipline or counseling for her husband, were explored—even though she wrote that her husband was a highly respected *leader* in their church.

Dobson is not the only prominent evangelical who takes wife-beating so lightly. In an interaction recorded and transcribed from the tape entitled Bible Questions and Answers Part 16, the following question was asked by a member of Grace Community Church in Sun Valley, California and answered by the pastor, Dr. John MacArthur Jr. **"How does a Christian woman react and deal with being a battered wife?"**

In answering this question, McArthur gave some very dangerous advice to battered wives. He said divorce is not an option to a battered wife, because the Bible doesn't permit it. MacArthur did say it was all right for the wife to get away while the pressure was on, but only with the perspective that she was *going to come back*. He warned wives to be very careful that they were not *provoking* the abusive situations. Because, he said, that was *very often the problem.*

Three years later, MacArthur said essentially the same thing (softened with a few disclaimers) in a booklet he still distributes today entitled "Answering Key Questions About the Family."

Dobson and McArthur seem to be on the same page when it comes to wife beating. How carelessly these two men, along with many other evangelical leaders, deal with the *lives* of women. Christian wives appear to be simply expendable in the name of good solid, patriarchal, male supremacist theology.

Statistics on domestic violence vary widely, but it is estimated that four to five million women are violently abused each year in this country alone. And it is documented by the FBI that over one thousand of them die. But in spite of the danger, there still seems to be a strong taboo within the Christian community against counseling women in abusive marriages to get out.

In addition to displaying a shocking lack of concern for the lives and physical safety of battered women, the so-called *scriptural* advice given by respected leaders such as Dobson and McArthur is also *sinful* advice. It is sin to attempt to control and manipulate another adult person's behavior (in some non-Christian circles this practice is called witchcraft). Only God is in a position to maneuver and manipulate righteously. The rest of us are called to control only one adult person's behavior—our own.

If leaders would spend only a fraction of the time they spend trying to teach women how to manipulate their husband's behavior through submission, teaching men how to control themselves, who knows how much tragedy could be averted?

Pastors and Christian leaders *must* become more sensitive and aggressive in learning to deal with the sin of abuse and domestic violence more effectively. The lives, health, and well-being of too many women depend on it.

A 1992 survey found that 15 to 20% of United Methodist women reported experiencing some type of physical violence from a boyfriend or husband.

In 2002, a report produced by the *Women's Network* and *The Family and Personal Relationships Committee to the Methodist Conference* stated that in a survey conducted by Roehampton University of Surrey, it was found that 1 in 4 female respondents reported experiencing domestic violence from a partner as an adult. In 53% of situations, the main perpetrators of domestic violence were husbands and male partners—which places the overall instance of wife abuse at about 1 in 8.

Assuming Methodists and United Methodists do not experience higher levels of domestic violence than other Christian groups, it would not be unreasonable to apply that ratio to other denominations as well. It is estimated that the top ten denominations in this country have *179,183,430* persons claiming to be affiliated with them. If that is the case, and if at least half of their adherents are female, then we have a total of one in eight of over *eighty nine million* Christian women who may have experienced some level of physical abuse by a boyfriend or husband.

Is that number too staggering to take seriously? Consider this. Surveys show that 50% of women who are physically abused *never* report the abuse or confide it to *anyone*. That means the statistics we do have reflect only *half* the violence that is actually taking place. And the statistics for the number of deaths attributed to domestic violence only reflect the number of *solved* murder cases. Do the math. We really are seeing only the tip of the iceberg.

With so much information on the subject at our disposal, how can the church continue to deny that spousal abuse and violence is not one of its more urgent issues?

It is a shame and reproach upon the church that one of the publicized goals of *secular* organizations is to engage *religious* leaders in the task of ending abuse.

What is wrong with this picture? In spite of overwhelming evidence that domestic violence is an issue even among Christians, evangelicals continue to dole out the same regurgitated platitudes that have been getting women killed for centuries. With so many women battered and murdered each year by their husbands or boyfriends, the passivity of the church in dealing realistically with this sin borders on criminal.

Not only is the evangelical church doing little to help the domestic violence situation among its adherents, the passive approach generally offered as a solution is, in actuality, *perpetuating* the problem—amounting to nothing less than church-sanctioned oppression.

Here are some of the *religious* aspects of the domestic violence problem as defined by *secular* sources:

- Christian women often feel *compelled* to stay in abusive relationships by scripture mandating them to "submit to their husbands" or "turn the other cheek."

- Rather than offering resources and alternatives to battered women, pastors, priests, imams and rabbis have often advised women to *return* to violent homes and be "better wives."

Is there really much evidence that the church is actively working to protect its women from domestic violence? If so, then why are *secular* organizations seeing a need to educate *religious* leaders on how to deal effectively with the issue?

Why isn't the church leading the charge on this one? Why isn't the church extending a helping hand to pull the abused to safety rather than using both hands to push her back into the danger zone? Why are men and women getting the same prejudicial pronouncements from church pulpits that they have been getting for centuries?

Men today are still being assured that God ordained them to rule over their wives, and women are still having it pounded into their psyches that their place is to submit to their husbands *regardless of the circumstances!*

Admittedly some progress is being made, but in spite of this, domestic violence remains a difficult theological issue. David and Anne Delaplane put together a manual for military chaplains entitled *The Spiritual Dimension In Victim Services*. According to the Delaplanes, the issue of submission of wives to husbands vs. marital separation is still critically important to religious leaders in any treatment of the subject of spousal/partner abuse. They report that some evangelical and fundamental clergy and congregations feel that to recommend that a woman who is being battered leave the home, obtain a restraining order, or file charges is in violation of the scriptural injunction for wives to obey their husbands.

Do the scriptures really require wives of batterers to become martyrs in their own homes? Are Christian wives truly forbidden by God to seek safety by leaving the "mission field" of their violent marriages?

Although the church has been largely responsible for encouraging women to take a strictly passive, reactionary approach to solving difficult marital issues, in the case of domestic violence, the *scriptures* espouse no such view. In fact, they clearly advise just the opposite.

It is very important for those who are in a position to offer support to a woman experiencing abuse from her husband to understand that, in this type of situation, the normal rules of engagement simply *do not apply*, and the scriptures do differentiate between winning an unbelieving spouse to the Lord and dealing with an abusive spouse.

Battered wives who are discouraged by their spiritual leadership from leaving their violent spouses are routinely directed to the New Testament passage of 1 Peter 3:1-2, where wives are told their unbelieving husbands might be converted to God by observing their chaste and obedient lifestyle. The problem with this is that these verses *do not* provide a scriptural basis for attempting to control and manipulate their husband's behavior.

Converting someone to the Lord and attempting to manipulate their behavior are two completely different things.

Nowhere in scripture can we find where an abused wife is told to respond reactively and passively to abuse.

Nor can we find a passage in which she is instructed to manipulate her husband's behavior. But we do find scripture in which she is instructed to do just the opposite. We find passages in which she is told to begin taking personal responsibility for her own physical safety and for deliverance from her abuser.

God's answer to oppression and abuse is always the same—*deliverance*. The scriptures clearly instruct the woman who is married to an abusive man to be proactive in her efforts to change her *situation*— never her spouse—and to take steps that will ensure both her present and future safety.

It is very important for the woman of faith to understand that it *is* God's will for her to make her physical safety, as well as her mental, emotional, and spiritual well-being a matter of paramount importance.

The scripture I am referring to is a passage that so radically changed my way of thinking concerning the abusive situation in my marriage, that it ultimately altered the course of my life. Understanding and utilizing the concepts found in this passage helped me obtain complete freedom from attitudes and perspectives that had contributed to my tolerating abuse for years.

Learning these truths was only a beginning, for obtaining my own personal freedom was a process. But the difference this new understanding made in my life has been profound and lasting.

The passage is found in Proverbs 2:10-13, and a close examination of it reveals God's heart and counsel to any person trapped in an abusive situation. A blueprint is found there for freedom from the cruel bondage of abuse.

> When wisdom entereth into thine heart, and knowledge is pleasant unto thy soul; Discretion shall preserve thee, understanding shall keep thee: to *deliver thee* from the way of *the evil man*, from the man that speaketh froward things; who leave the paths of uprightness, to walk in the ways of darkness;
>
> Proverbs 2:10-13

This is a power packed passage with an unmistakable message of freedom for *anyone* who is living a life of oppression at the hands of another human being—that includes the abused wife.

Verse 10 relays a key truth by saying, "When *wisdom* entereth into thine heart . . . "

Wisdom is the knowledge and ability to make the right choices at the right time, and one of the key words in this verse, aside from wisdom, is '*when*.' Our creator is well aware of the tendency of the abused wife to process the facts of her life in such a way that she can more easily live with them. The daughter of Eve often looks for an underlying positive aspect to her situation and makes excuses for her abuser's behavior. She tends to agree with modern psychology by attributing his abuse to motivations other than sheer selfishness and cruelty. To contemplate otherwise would be to invite an avalanche of heartache and emotional pain into a life that is already filled to capacity with it.

Because of this tendency, she does not easily acquire the knowledge and ability to make the right choices at the right time. Nevertheless, God does hold each of us personally responsible for having hearts that are ready to receive his wisdom.

The second part of Verse 10 speaks of *knowledge* becoming pleasant to our soul. The Hebrew word translated into knowledge in this verse means knowing, learning, or *alertness* (seeing things as they really are). And one of the key words in this passage is still "when."

Don't we women love to look through rose-colored glasses that show the beauty and *hide the truth*— those amazing glasses that allow us to see the hearts and motives of our beloved abusers as we would like them to be rather than how they really are?

We must take them off.

Perceiving the raw truth of our situations must stop being abhorrent to us! We must allow God's wisdom to enter into our hearts and knowledge must become pleasant to our souls.

As painful as it may be, we must accept that seeing things as they really are is preferable to living
in a fantasy world of our own creation—in a world
that *does not exist*. Sound decisions and responsible
choices cannot be made if we stubbornly cling to our
beloved fantasies.

Verse 11 tells us that discretion shall preserve us.
One of the meanings of the Hebrew word translated
as "discretion" in this verse is *a carefully thought-
out plan*. There we have it, straight from the word of
God, that if we expect safety and protection, we must
proactively participate in it. Planning our own preservation is not being underhanded or disloyal.

Verse 11 goes on to say that understanding will *keep*
us. In this passage, the biblical definition of the word
"understanding" means intelligence—the ability to
separate mentally, and to be perceptive. *Keep*, in this
verse, means to guard and protect. Acquiring this
perceptiveness, which gives us the ability to separate
truth from lies, brings much protection to the woman
in an abusive relationship where words and actions
often wildly disagree.

Verse 12 goes on to tell us why it is so important that
we acquire these skills. It is so we can be *delivered*
from the evil man.

It *is* God's will that we be delivered from the evil
man, and it is critically important to understand this

fact when the inevitable pain and confusion sets in during the decisionmaking process.

Another crucial fact that needs to be understood is that, according to scripture, it is *behavior*—not intentions—that designates a person as either good or evil. I had developed the habit of excusing my former husband's abusive behavior by reasoning that he was a really a good person who just *behaved* badly at times. But according to Proverbs 2:12-13, the evil man is defined by his *behavior*.

The King James Bible uses the Old English word "froward" to describe the evil man. This is a very descriptive word that includes several shades of meaning. It has got to be a one of a kind word, and it is a shame we do not use it anymore. It means perversity, fraud, change, to the contrary, *tortuous*.

Doesn't that accurately sum up the various aspects of an abuser? Doesn't the abusive man typically say one thing now and another thing later—always tortuously keeping the tension levels high? Doesn't he seem to glory in keeping his victim a confused, off balance, emotional *wreck*? Indeed, doesn't it seem to be a validating experience for him?

The Word of God tells us that when we have the knowledge and ability to make the right choices at the right time, when we are ready to take off the rose-colored glasses, when we truly prefer to see things as they really are as opposed to how we would like them to be, *then* a carefully thought out plan, along with perceptiveness and the ability to separate the truth from lies, will guard, protect and *deliver* us from the evil man.

Taking steps to ensure our own safety is not demonstrating a sinful lack of faith in God's life-changing power on behalf of our mate. Only God knows who will ultimately surrender to a life-changing repentance from evil behavior and who will not.

Battered wives cannot afford to focus on the unscriptural goal of *changing their husband's behavior*. The price can be too high. Too many women have been strung along, indefinitely, with the carrot of false hope dangling before their eyes and have ended up paying for this hope with the ruination of their *entire* lives. Too many women have *lost* their lives. It is better not to gamble with this one. It's not worth it—*and God does not require it.*

A Life Consumed

Kathy Hartman

"My Daughter stayed with her
husband . . . and it cost her her
life. It led to the apparent taking of
her own life. She suffered terrible
verbal, as well as physical, abuse
for almost twenty-four years.
It is fatal if allowed to run its
course. . ."

Grief-Stricken Mother
Quoted from, *Battered Into Submission*,
James and Phyllis Alsdurf, 1989

Kathy Hartman Isler

They have stricken me . . .

They have beaten me . . .

I will seek it yet again.

The Holy Bible

6

Oh My God—I'm an Addict!

Who is this that comes up from the wilderness leaning on her beloved?

The Holy Bible

As a woman of faith who was in love with an abusive husband I would read that verse in Song of Solomon and yearn for the day my beloved would be transformed from a cruel, abusive creature into a gentle and loving companion.

I absolutely knew that would happen. I saw in that verse a promise I could sink my teeth into. I could latch my faith onto it—be obsessed with it, and it would be pleasing to God, because it was his Word I was clinging to. . . . *Or was it*?

Were my eyes set on God and his powerful Word—or were they solidly fixed on something else—on some*one* else? Who was I worshipping? Who was I really living for?

I had to face these questions and answer them honestly. It wasn't easy.

Now it's your turn.

- Is your mind held captive by an abuser who does not seem to return your obsession—or at least returns it only when he feels he has gone too far and knows you are ready to walk?

- Does the pain in your heart, the anguish of your mind, and the loneliness you experience at times seem almost too much to bear?

- Have you worn out friends and family, tiring them through hearing the woes of your abusive marriage or relationship?

- Have you withdrawn from friends and family and avoided developing new friendships because you have grown weary of experiencing the contempt aimed at those who just can't seem to *get it together*?

Are you ready for relief?

Relief *can* be found. There *is* a solution. The question is, are you willing to find relief God's way—or will you cave and allow yourself to believe that the occasional (and usually very brief) honeymoon will be permanent this time?

Will you seek just "one more" temporary fix just to see if, this time, it won't turn out differently and fix everything permanently?

Does it sound as if I am addressing an addict?

Consider this, one of the first things alcoholics learn when they attend an Alcoholics Anonymous (*AA*) meeting is the definition of insanity. Now why would a definition of insanity be relevant to an alcoholic? An alcoholic is not insane— just addicted. However, *AA* insists that the person addicted to alcohol exhibits insane behavior. The *AA* definition of insanity is "doing the same thing over and over again *expecting different results.*"

Haven't we, as battered and formerly battered women done the same thing? Haven't we rehearsed the same scenes over and over, each time expecting things to somehow turn out differently? Haven't we refused to throw in the towel because *this time* things really might get better?

Those who tolerate abuse from a spouse on a long term basis are most likely addicted . . . to a *person.*

Many of you are likely already protesting this analysis, saying, "I am not addicted to my husband! I *love* him." Before slamming the book shut, let's make a few comparisons. The dictionary definition of love is a feeling of strong personal attachment, ardent affection, unselfish, loyal, and benevolent concern for the good of another.

That about sizes it up doesn't it? That's a *good* thing isn't it—to love another person unselfishly?

Now let's look at the definition of addiction. Addiction means to devote, to apply habitually one's mind to . . . to give one's self up or over to. . . .

Hmmm . . . that could apply as well, couldn't it?

Over time in an abusive marriage or relationship, real, God-given love can begin to take on the characteristics of Satan's counterfeit of addiction. That does not mean the real love is no longer there. It just means that very real aspects of addiction have entered into the equation and can very easily become the dominant factor in the relationship.

Addiction is very similar in nature to a romantic relationship. Ask any alcoholic or addict. They will confirm this. Addicts yearn for their beloved constantly. When they are not together, they will go to almost any length to find, and be with, their beloved. That is their only goal; *nothing* else matters.

They know their beloved is destroying their life, but they cannot, or will not, give them up. The time they spend together seems almost fulfilling . . . and so full of promise . . . so promising in fact, that the pain of the rest of the relationship seems worth that short, periodic, *temporary* fix.

The major difference between those who are addicted to a substance and those who are addicted to a person is that substance abusers *know* their beloved will never be anything more to them than a temporary solution. They know that, in the final analysis, their beloved will let them down. They understand and freely acknowledge the destructive nature of the relationship. They know it will never get any better. They make their choices with their eyes wide open.

Not so for those who are addicted to a person. We hold on, with our very lives, to the hope that our beloved abuser will miraculously transform into the caring, compassionate companion we want, need, and believe they can become. We not only wear rose-colored glasses that distort the present, but these incredible glasses actually allow us to see into the future—a future of *our own* design—one we like so much, we decide to leave the present behind altogether and move there permanently.

This is a much more insidious addiction than drugs or alcohol ever could be because it so thoroughly blinds us to the reality of our present situations and of what our real needs are—needs that no temporary fix can ever fulfill.

Is your marriage or relationship nothing more than a series of temporary fixes? Are you living from peak to peak, honeymoon to honeymoon with nothing but abuse (or physical violence), heartache, longing, and loneliness in between?

If this is the case, then it is time to go into rehab—Jesus' rehab. It is time to experience the withdrawal and go through the wall. It is time to come up from the wilderness leaning on your beloved—and Beloved, *that is not easy.* But it is so worth it!

How does Jesus' rehab work?

First realize that only one person can help you. That person is Jesus. Support persons and systems are important, helpful and absolutely necessary. Allow your friends to be there for you. Seek out your friends to help you through this difficult time. But realize this, they *cannot* make it better. Only Jesus can make it better.

Second, be willing to go through the withdrawal.

Withdrawal is painful. DT's set in—then comes the finale, when it seems as if you cannot take anymore. The pain, loneliness, and uncertainty become almost unbearable. It hurts, it's scary—but do not reach for that temporary fix! *Refuse to be comforted by the counterfeit.* Do not lean on that broken reed that will only pierce your hand. Lean instead on Jesus. He promises to walk with you. Cry on his shoulder. Pour out all your pain, grief, fears and frustrations to him. He's listening. He cares. And he can, *and will,* make it better.

The pain *must* be experienced—fully—and without anesthesia. Give it to the Lord. Trust him with it.

Take a firm grip on his hand and walk through the wall with him. You will emerge on the other side a different person . . . a stronger person . . . a person who understands the faithfulness and the power of your God.

You will come up from the wilderness leaning on your beloved—who you will now know . . . *is Jesus*.

~ ~ ~

I have been there, and I am there no longer. I have been to Jesus' rehab. I have walked through the wall with him, and I promise—Jesus *can* make it better.

One day runs into the next. You feel **numb** on the inside. Things seem **vague** and **obscure**, and your long ago dreams and ambitions turn into an **ENDLESS** and **perpetual roller coaster of pain and heartache.** You watch as you and your family are systematically destroyed piece by piece, bit by bit. Nothing fits together anymore, and your household walks on eggshells . . . in hopes of not provoking the abuser once again.

Those hopes are false hopes, my friend.

Kathy Isler

The House on Taft Street

An overwhelming sadness and regret encompassed me as I turned to look at the house . . . for the last time.

To the left, the cockleshells bobbed at the edge of the pond. To the right, miles of prairie where the graceful grasses quivered and swayed and the calendulas nodded in the capricious Kansas wind.

Along the path, the buddleia reached for the sun, their flowers a mass of oranges and yellows as butterflies danced across their heads.

I felt my heart leap as the intangible aura of the house beckoned me to relinquish my resolve . . . and return to the solitude and decay within its bowels.

I thrust out my hand as if to ward off the actual experience of being drawn inside once again.

A tear rolled down my cheek at the thought of all the blessings yearned for those many years, but never really known.

I felt the ache in my soul and the abrasive scrape of the spiritual fracture I knew I must exchange for a new life away from all that was familiar.

It was finally over . . . All those years of pain . . . The fault, I thought, was mine.

I must be strong to seek out and discover new ways to live life.

As I looked at the house, it was like looking in a mirror, reflecting what seemed to be a stranger.

I reached out to touch the brick wall and felt the malignant hum of the house course through my body. "No! No." I thought, "No more."

The family clique within its walls was mine no longer. Children grown . . . my part here was done.

This house, once a perfect dream, an ornament of silver and bronze within my mind's eye, held so many painful memories . . . it was time now for me to leave . . . To seek out a new life.

I turned and walked away for the last time—never looking back.

There was still time I thought, time to laugh, time to cry . . .

A time to love again . . .

A time to start anew.

Kathy Isler © 1997

The Fragrance Of Grief

Emergence

7

Journey from Fear to Peace

Fear not, for I am with thee. . . .

The Holy Bible

A few years back, one of my former co-workers (I'll call her Mary) confided to me that her husband was threatening to leave her if she didn't break off a friendship with a female friend she enjoyed spending time with. When I asked her if the friendship was interfering with her marriage in any way, she insisted it was not. Mary said her husband consistently objected to her being close to *anyone*—including her own family members—and he excused this by telling her he was only "looking out for her."

Mary's situation hit very close to home with me, as I was going through the same thing in my own marriage. Although my husband was no support to me at all, he objected to any source of personal support I might turn to besides him.

Like me, Mary recognized her husband's overt efforts to control her through his threats to leave, but she did not seem to be catching on to his covert efforts. She was not seeing through the camouflage of his criticism of anyone she was close to. She seemed to want to believe he really was concerned that she might be "taken advantage of."

As I said, I was struggling with these same issues in my marriage, but I had already recognized that my husband was attempting to maintain control over me by keeping me isolated from my family and by deliberately attempting to undermine and destroy any friendships I might forge. I could also admit he was succeeding in his efforts to an alarming degree.

As a Bible believing Christian, I had no desire to dishonor Jesus by dishonoring my husband. But did honoring my husband really include giving up friends and family that I loved and needed, just to cater to his fears and please his ego? I did not believe so, but as difficult as he was to live with, I loved him. And the fear of losing him ranked very high on my fear meter.

My journey from fear to peace was a long and painful one. And I do not know of any short cuts. I can only share from my own experience that when I finally reached the point of saturation—the point at which I could tolerate no more fear or pain—I finally became willing to give up my methods of dealing with the problems within my marriage and allowed God to begin teaching me his. It was then that I began desperately crying out to God for new direction—and, as always, he answered me.

It was not the answer I was looking for. But it was definitely the answer I needed. It was at that point in my life that I discovered God's blueprint for freedom—Proverbs 2:10-13 (covered in detail in chapter five). I knew God had spoken to me through this passage of scripture. And after studying it closely, I began to understand what truly remarkable and concise direction it gave. I knew I had reached a turning point in my life, and if I could learn to implement the instruction I had just received, I could be free, forever, from the torment of indecision and from fear of losing my spouse.

That passage helped me understand that when I became willing to see and do things God's way instead of my way, I would be cared for by God and would no longer be at the mercy of abusive treatment or threats of abandonment.

Did that understanding solve the problems within my marriage? No. Did I immediately run out and file for divorce? To my family's everlasting dismay, no, I did not. It took quite some time for me to firmly grasp the fact that I had to let go of the wheel. I had to give up control. I had to stop trying to figure everything out.

Is that a surprising statement coming from one who was trying to escape *being* controlled? It shouldn't. Everyone has to have some sense that they are in control of some portion of their lives. One of my ways of feeling in control of that chaotic situation was by not admitting defeat. I simply refused to give up. I was constantly trying to figure out ways to fix things. I was even using prayer to try and control the situation. That was wrong.

It was with great difficulty that I reached the painful conclusion that my efforts to change my beloved abuser might be fruitless. And I finally, reluctantly, became willing to accept the consequence of divorce or permanent separation if that became necessary.

I would like to stop here and say that I am not advocating divorce as an across-the-board solution for all marriages with these types of problems. I am saying though, that, painful as it may be, the possibility of divorce or permanent separation must become a viable option to the abused or battered wife. The *possibility* of divorce or permanent separation must cease to become the unthinkable, if she ever hopes to be free from fear of these things.

We cannot be threatened by things we do not fear.

Over the next few years, through many separations and reconciliations, I made repeated sincere efforts to save my marriage, but my efforts finally boiled down to simply trying to free myself emotionally, physically, and legally from my husband.

I admit there were many occasions when I initiated a separation in an effort to manipulate my husband into seeking professional help. Did it work? Sometimes—temporarily. Other times I left in an effort to be free from him forever. Did that work? Over a period of time—yes.

There are those who still criticize me for loving my abusive husband and "wasting" years of my life trying to make that marriage work. The following are a few of the questions I wrestled with as I struggled to find some sanity and God-given solutions to the chaos that filled my life, and some conclusions I finally came to:

- Is it ok for an abused wife to love her husband? Yes.
- Is it ok to want to make the marriage work? Yes.
- Is it ok to leave if the abuse escalates? Yes.
- Is it ok to return and try again? As much as I would love to say, "*No! Stay away,*" the answer to that question has to be yes as well.

Can any of us definitively say that it is *always* the will of God for an abused wife to leave her husband permanently? No, we cannot. But we *can* definitively say that if she acknowledges God in all her ways, he *will* direct her paths. We *can* definitively say we know it is within the parameters of God's perfect will, as revealed in his written word, for an abused wife to proactively seek ways to protect herself from assault and abuse.

We can assure an abused wife that it is not okay to be motivated, coerced, and seemingly driven into returning by fear, guilt, false hope, and confusion. The scriptures tell us the wisdom that comes from above (from God) is peaceable, gentle, and easy to be received. God leads. He does not drive. And he is *not* the author of confusion.

But if a woman is acknowledging God in all her ways, and feels the Holy Spirit is directing her path and leading her not to end her marriage, or even continue with a separation—as much as that may gall the rest of us—her choices need to be acknowledged as valid. She may indeed be following the leading of the Holy Spirit. Who are we to say she is not?

In my case, though, I eventually reached the point where I could deal with the possibility of losing my husband without the fear and pain it had previously produced. I accepted the fact that he might never change. That in turn made it possible for me to take off the rose-colored glasses and see my marriage for what it really was, rather than how I wanted to see it.

I came to realize the fine-tuner on my discernment apparatus had become damaged due to constant exposure to abuse. As the fear abated, it began working again, and I began seeing things differently. In addition to the overt abuse, I found the covert and more subtle abuse in our marriage coming into sharper focus. For the first time in a very long time I was seeing things clearly. I could honestly face the fact that I had developed a tolerance for the abuse and could admit that I had been accepting much of it without challenge.

In defense of myself, along with other battered and abused wives, I must add this. There were many times when, even though I acutely felt the unacceptability of his abusive behavior, I was so exhausted from the battle that I consciously allowed many things to pass unchallenged rather than face his wrath in dealing with them. In addition to fearing his explosive temper, I had reached a point in dealing with the abuse where I deliberately saved my strength for the bigger things. If I contested everything abusive, I would have been engaging in constant verbal skirmishes, and I simply did not have the energy for that—other times, it simply was not physically safe for me to contend.

Overall, refusing to allow my life to revolve around this man I loved so much, and accepting the fact that he might not change, were the first steps I took to freeing myself from the fear of loss that had been a huge factor in keeping me bound to the relationship.

I was finally able to *let him go.*

It hurt. I continued for a long time to love him, hope for the best, and seek solutions to the abuse in our marriage, but I gave my hopes for the marriage, along with the fear of losing him, to God. I concentrated on acknowledging God in all of *my* ways so he could direct *my* paths. I could not do this for my husband. And I found myself growing, and resting, in the knowledge that wherever God took me, even if it was away from my husband, it would surely be to a place that was good for me.

Was the journey painful and difficult? Yes.
Was it worth it? Yes.
Do I have peace? Yes!

Shreds

Kathy Hartman

Perhaps we don't look like SHREDS on the outside, but that's how we feel inside. We are torn apart emotionally, we're confused. . . . "Why is this happening? Why is he doing this? What's wrong with me? What did I do?" We're physically tired, we're terrified. Those of us who have children are terrified for them as well. . . .

Kathy Isler

8

Navigating the Minefield

O Lord, I know that the way of man is not in himself; it is not in man that walketh to direct his steps.

The Holy Bible

An abusive relationship is like a minefield; it is full of hidden explosives.

In navigating the minefield of an abusive marriage or relationship, there is only one way to do it successfully: that is to acknowledge God in all our ways, so he can direct our paths (Proverbs 3:6 KJV).

His help is needed to avoid the pitfalls and survive the explosives. His help is needed to tell truth from lies, and His help is needed to know His perfect will in times of extreme distress and confusion.

On one of the many occasions when I fled from my nightmare of a marriage, I found myself driving in a blinding thunderstorm. The storm raging outside my car was nothing compared to the storm raging within my heart. With tears streaming down my face, I cried out my pain and frustration to God. I did not know what to do or where to go. My Bible lay on the passenger seat beside me, and I reached over as I drove and flipped it open. The storm in my heart was instantly calmed as my eyes fell upon the words of Psalm 142:3, *"When my spirit was overwhelmed within me, then thou knewest my path."*

I did not have a clue where I was going, but God did. And that was all that really mattered. His Word gave me assurance that he was able to get me from point "A" to point "B," even when I had no idea where point "B" was.

To the person who does not have faith in Jesus Christ, that might sound unbelievable—even irresponsible, but to the Christian it should not. There are times when even our most well-laid plans and expectations can fall through. These times are sometimes engineered by God in order to build more faith in those of us who are called to be people of faith. So why should it seem unbelievable that we can be in the perfect will of God even in situations that may be completely unexpected, unplanned, and appear to be completely out of control?

I had occasion to learn a little more about the faithfulness and providence of God when I reached the point where I wasn't trying to "fix it" anymore. I had decided I was leaving "for good this time" and tore out of my driveway amid a hailstorm of abuse. With tires spinning and little more than the clothes on my back, I headed for the home of a family member that had always been a safe haven for me. But when I arrived, the circumstances within that "haven" had changed. I found myself an unwelcome guest with no job, very little money, and a roof over my head that I could count on for only about another twenty-four hours.

But God had gone ahead of me, and without my saying a word to anyone to about my dilemma, I was offered a safe, comfortable place to live until I could find a job, get on my feet, and make some critical decisions about my future.

It is a credit to those who extended their love to me at that time that it was completely unconditional. They did not insist that I promise "never to go back" in exchange for their hospitality. They simply opened their door in true Christian love. They said I had a place with them as long as I needed one, and they remained true to their word.

Should we, as Christians, advise a wife who is suffering from physical violence to get out of a potentially dangerous situation? Absolutely! But once she is safe, what we cannot, and should not, do is try and tell her what God's perfect will is for her life.

Knowing the perfect will of God is very important to many battered/abused Christian wives. The committed Christian woman needs to know with certainty that she is not stepping away from the will of God as she makes the critical and difficult decisions that are required of her. And there is only one way she can do that. She must trust the faithful promise of God that if she will acknowledge him in all her ways—he will direct her paths (Proverbs 3:6 KJV).

The road to resolution or dissolution of an abusive marriage is winding and rocky, with many smoke-screens, pitfalls and ambushes along the way. The abuser will more than likely be dishonest, and make every effort to manipulate the situation so as to re-store the balance of the relationship back to where he wants it—which is him being in complete control. And as difficult as it is for the uninitiated to imagine, charm and guilt are two of his most effective weap-ons in achieving this end.

Yes, wife-beaters can be very charming. And if charm does not work, contrary to the unsubstantiated claims of James Dobson concerning their lack of communi-cation skills, studies overwhelmingly conclude abu-sive men are master communicators and experts at making their *victims* feel guilty!

How does the Christian wife withstand her husband's completely believable, often tearful pleas for forgive-ness and just *"one more chance?"* Sometimes she doesn't. But if she is successful in withstanding the charm and the tears, her husband will often apply, next, to her Christian conscience.

After all, doesn't the Bible command her to love and *forgive*? He swears he needs her help if there is any hope of a change, and how can she help him change if she leaves? If charm and guilt both fail, he usually resorts back to what almost always gets him what he wants — anger, threats, and violence.

The *most dangerous time* in the life of a battered woman is when she is attempting to leave her husband. The extreme danger of this time cannot be overly stressed or underestimated. Pastors, counselors, friends and family of the abused, *please*, do not forget this fact when called upon for help in these situations.

75% of battered women, who are killed by their husbands, die while trying to escape the abuse.

That is why a carefully thought-out plan is so very important. It is not a betrayal for a battered wife to carefully and *secretly* plan her escape. I remember lying in the emergency room, beaten almost beyond recognition, feeling *guilt* (!) upon hearing what my wife-beating husband said when he realized I had gone "behind his back" and called for help while he was out of the house. His response to the news was, "She betrayed me."

*Note to battered wives: I am convinced the Holy Spirit of God inserted the words of Proverbs chapter two into the Holy Scriptures with *you* in mind. He was very clear

that following his instructions would result in the preservation of *your* life.

It is *not* recommended that you attempt to sit down with your violent husband and try to reasonably explain why you feel you must leave. It is also not recommended that you precipitate any sort of crisis before leaving in order to shock your husband into seeing a need for change. The goal here is **not** *to change your husband's behavior*. It is to preserve what is left of **your** life—possibly even to *save* your life.

The committed Christian woman's only hope of having peace of mind during all this is to know, without a doubt, that she is making the right choices at any given point in time. And the only way she can know that is by following the instructions given in Proverbs 3:6, "*Acknowledge him in all thy ways* (word, thought and deed), *and he shall direct thy paths*." Only then can she be assured that she is in the center of God's will and that he truly is directing her paths.

Might it be within the perfect will of God for there to be separations and reconciliations along the way? Of course it might.

Are there guarantees in the Word of God that if Proverbs 3:6 is scrupulously followed, the abuser will miraculously see the havoc and destruction he is causing and allow repentance, deliverance, and transformation to come into his own life?

No, there are no such guarantees.

The guarantee is this, if we will acknowledge God in all of *our* ways, *our* paths will be directed. And the path *God* sets us on always results in our good . . . even if that path is steep, rocky, and painful at times.

The Problem of wife abuse is not one of feminism, secular humanism, or a lack of headship in the home—it is the problem of evil—unseen and unopposed.

James & Phyllis Alsdurf
Battered Into Submission, 1989

Myth:

"The abused is most likely a victim of past abuse and will ultimately gravitate towards another abusive situation . . . stay far **_far_** away from this situation— you have no idea what you are getting yourself into."

Anonymous typical attitude 2005

9

Don't Be a Broken Reed

"That broken reed . . . on which if you lean, it will pierce your hand."

The Holy Bible

"Why did you let him come back?!"

"Don't come crawling to me again!"
"Are you going to go back?"
"You two need to *get it together.*"

These are a few of the responses I received from some of the miserable comforters in my own life and even from those whose job it was to protect me — the police. The abused / battered woman is very familiar with these attitudes, and the tragedy is that she has probably encountered them so frequently, she will often not ask for help until her situation becomes very desperate. And in her desperation, these are things she is likely to hear.

I once bought a bus ticket for a total stranger—no questions asked. I then offered her a safe place, along with a noncritical listening ear, to wait for the bus. So what if chances were good she would return to her abuser within a very short period of time? I wasn't willing, that day, to allow someone to go back into a situation that may have cost her her life. And who's to say that an unconditional helping hand from a total stranger might not have had some lasting, positive, effect on her life?

What did I have to lose by extending my hands and heart freely to this woman? What did it really cost me? One afternoon of my time—and green stuff . . . you know, the stuff we can't take with us?

After experiencing that final, brutal, assault described in chapter one, I remember not wanting to call my pastor for help, because he had exhibited quite a bit of impatience and condescension towards me when I had called him on an earlier occasion. It is a good thing I overcame that initial reluctance, because he and his wife were the only ones geographically close enough to get me away quickly—which they gladly did. I remain very grateful for their unquestioning, immediate response to my call that afternoon. But I could just as easily have caved to the shame and growing resentment resulting from a previous, more callous, response. If I had, would I even be alive to-day? I will never know the answer to that question . . . because I did call.

We should be aware of how harmful our attitudes

can be to someone who is hurting and may be in real danger. The possibility is very real that we could be in contact with a battered/abused wife and not even know it. Some researchers believe the number of women who experience physical abuse by their husbands is as high as 1 of every 2—50%!

I remember settling into a new church some years back. I was really enjoying getting to know the people there. My husband was very abusive. Life at home was a veritable hell on earth, and I desperately needed some positive relationships and social activities in my life. After just a few weeks of attending the new church, the inevitable happened, and I found myself separated, *again*, from my husband. I let the cat out of the bag during a telephone conversation with one of the ladies. She had called to invite me to a class get-together at her home. We were chatting, as women do, and I confided in her that my husband and I had separated. I did not tell her about the abuse—only that we were separated.

Her response to the news absolutely floored me. I quickly hung up the phone and did not bother going to her "get-together." When she heard that my husband and I had separated, without knowing a single detail, instead of offering me friendship, a shoulder to cry on, or some conversation over a cup of coffee, she offered me . . . *counseling!*

She was obviously very taken with the fact that she

and her husband were part of the Church's counseling staff.

Admittedly, there is a time and place for counseling, but when a person is hurting due to a recent loss such as separation from a spouse, offering your time and a friendly ear to listen is a much more needed and appropriate initial gesture.

True friends are a rarity among any group of people, and sadly, among Christians they seem to be just about as scarce as anywhere else. In my experience, unless someone is involved with *our* church, *our* group, or *our* project, no one seems to have time for them. That proves doubly true for the abused woman who cannot seem to "get it together" and who does not seem to fit in anywhere. No one *really* wants to know about her problems. But how can we be a true friend to the battered woman, and help bear her burdens with her (as the scriptures command), unless we are willing to love her and *get involved*?

Here is something to think about for those who may be reluctant to offer compassion, friendship and support to a battered woman: the average alcoholic or drug addict has a largely self-inflicted problem. But isn't the drug addict or alcoholic worthy of our compassion?

Many may not agree that they are, but the vast number of ministries, social agencies and shelters that exist in order to assist alcoholics, chemical substance abusers, and even the homeless on their road to recovery and social stability, is a testament to the fact that there are many who do.

However, it is a sad fact that there are more *animal* shelters in this country than there are shelters for battered women, in spite of the fact that 50% of the female homeless population is homeless due to domestic violence.

Something else we should consider is this: even though there are definite similarities between the behavior of battered women towards their abusers and addicts towards their drugs, the response of friends and family to the situations should be completely different.

It is a well known fact that keeping our doors open to alcoholics and drug addicts usually only enables them to continue in their destructive lifestyles. But keeping an open door to a battered woman has just the opposite effect. It *strengthens* her (even if it does not seem like it at the time) in the process of making the decision to take proactive steps toward improving her situation.

I understand that it is almost always a frustrating and frightening process—and it is a process—for anyone who may be attempting to assist a battered woman. At one Victims' Assistance office, I was told the average battered woman does not leave her situation permanently until after an average of eight reported assaults (usually severe assaults), and frustrated family and friends may have been involved in the aftermath of, or at least heard about, many of the unreported assaults.

But the good news is that many battered women are able to find their way out. And when they do, they have the capability of becoming a force to be reckoned with.

I came face to face with this fact when I found out the director of the Victims Assistance Office I found myself sitting in was a former battered wife herself.

We all answer to God for our choices, and we are all responsible for acknowledging him in all of our ways so he can direct our paths. At the very least, compassion and *respect* should be extended as we offer emotional support or attempt to assist the battered woman in finding resources that can help her.

No More!

How long have you stayed, one year, five, ten, twenty? When will you find yourself saying **NO MORE!** It took me over twenty years.

Kathy Isler

10

The Marriage That May Not Survive

I do not know if testimonies about the miraculous intervention of God in violent marriages abound, but I do know they exist. I remember being very moved by the story of a couple that experienced the transforming power of God in their marriage, and the violence ended permanently . . . after they divorced.

It turned out they met again, a few years after completely losing touch with one another, fell instantly in love and remarried. During the years they had been out of touch with one another, God had done an amazing work in transforming the life of the previously violent husband, and the second time around the marriage was very happy.

They give God great praise and glory for this. And they should. He deserves it.

I am certain there are more testimonies such as this

one, but—and I must insert a very big "but" here—
that does *not* happen in *most* cases.

Please do not slam the book shut on me! I have not
just blasphemed God. I have simply stated a fact.

Most abusers never change.

Are we afraid God's reputation as an all powerful
problem-solver-life-changer will be tarnished by acknowledging that fact?

It is not God's fault when a person chooses not to do
the right thing. And even He acknowledges, in his
Word, that there are those who will never submit to
His will for their lives. But might there be a God-
given solution for the victim of an abusive spouse
other than remaining in the home or marriage?

The answer to that question has been difficult for
evangelicals to agree on. But while the theologians
are busy debating, women's lives are being wasted,
ruined, and lost.

While the theologians of Jesus' day debated about
whether it was scripturally correct to heal on the Sabbath day—Jesus healed a man. Jesus said Sabbath or
no—this man needs relief.

When King David's men were hungry on the Sabbath

day, he threw the theologians into a tizzy by picking corn! And Jesus said he was justified in doing that—because *lives* are more important than theology.

In the scriptures, liars are held in low esteem and even told their souls are imperiled. But the Hebrew midwives in Egypt didn't think twice about lying to save the lives of condemned infants.

I am not advocating lying or deliberately sinning. But I am saying, without apology, that *lives* are the most important thing. And if a choice needs to be made between saving a life or making certain that we are making a theologically correct decision, *go for the life every time.*

And don't forget, in an abusive or violent marriage, the rules *do **not** apply* . . . for the simple reason that one of the members of the marriage does not acknowledge the rules as applying to him. Physical violence is *against the law*, yet the wife-beater breaks the law. He sees one law for himself and another law for everyone else. If he disdains civil law, what makes us think the laws of God will mean anything to him?

Could professional counseling help? It might—if the batterer would seek it. He rarely does. What about pastoral counseling? Many abusers are professing Christians. They are often active in their churches. Some are *Pastors* in their churches. Some might be willing to seek pastoral counseling. But are most pastors qualified to deal with abusive situations? In my personal experience, no, they are not.

I sought help from both pastors and licensed counselors. *None* of the pastors I approached (and only one of the licensed counselors) were qualified to deal with the problems in my marriage. And none gave me any advice that I found helpful in navigating the situation.

I had been doing much research into the subject myself, and received acknowledgements from more than one of them that I probably knew more about the dynamics of such a relationship than they did. It truly is a dark arena. One counselor even admitted to being intimidated by such a knowledgeable client.

I was told more than once there was no hope for my marriage (who besides God knew that?), and one of them came right out and blamed me for the abuse. She said I had trained my husband to be abusive—she probably learned that from listening to Drs. Minirth and Meier's Christian Psychology Radio Clinic on Moody radio, or by reading their book, *Happiness Is a Choice*, which places the blame squarely on the battered wife for the fact that her husband beats her.

Time and again, I was put on the defensive by the very ones I went to for help—they **_all_** wanted to know *why I stayed* (sound familiar?).

In seeking a counselor for such a marriage, experienced, professional, counsel *for the abuser* must be sought—not a marriage counselor for the *couple*. Marriage counseling for couples will not work in a domestic violence situation—at least not at first. It is essential that someone well trained, with a successful track record in working with abusers be sought.

I do not usually recommend that Christians seek counseling from non-Christian counselors, but in this case, if a qualified Christian counselor cannot be found, I make an exception. The reason for this is, we are dealing with physical violence—*assault.* Women can and do *die* from being assaulted by their husbands. We are talking about saving lives. Even if the batterer is a professing Christian, he is demonstrating absolutely no regard for what God says about his behavior. He is rebelling against God by living a lifestyle contrary to biblical teachings. He is breaking the law. He is wreaking havoc and destruction on every life that is within his sphere of influence. If there is no qualified Christian counselor available and a non-Christian counselor has demonstrated an ability to help abusers see the attitudes that lead to such destruction and can help them change their behavior—and possibly help save a life and a family—I say go for it.

Studies do show that the safety of battered wives often improves while the batterer is participating in a batterer prevention program, and what is there to prevent God from doing a transforming work in someone's life through a secular program? Who is to say this may not be the vehicle God chooses for some?

Unfortunately, even with counseling, most abusers are reluctant to seek real change. They often attend counseling sessions only under extreme pressure, such as their wife leaving or a court order, and are really only seeking a way to restore the status quo back to where they want it—which is their wife living in the home and them in complete control.

My abusive husband received court ordered counseling. It helped. He attended group sessions for three months, but he refused to continue past the time ordered by the court. Within two weeks of discontinuing counseling, he returned to his former abusive behavior. For us, the batterer's intervention program was only a temporary remedy. However, I do not rule out the possibility that someone else might experience more lasting results than my spouse did. Admittedly, though, my faith in counseling as a solution to marital violence is minimal.

It turns out that professional studies in Florida agree with me on this. Follow-up studies have shown no difference at all in the numbers of men who re-assault their wives as compared to those ordered into programs or those just getting probation. Other studies conclude that, overall, there is some success among batterers who *complete* the programs. The catch is getting them to complete the programs—48% drop out. Findings reveal most of the success takes place while the abusive men are actively attending weekly sessions, but many quickly relapse into violent behavior when the counseling is discontinued.

Arrest and prosecution have been proven, by far, to be the best method in deterring violence.

So what about the marriage that may not survive? If a marriage does not survive, does that mean God failed, or the victim failed or somehow misunderstood God's direction for her life? No. It means that a man exercised his own free will and made his own destructive choices.

None of us can cause another person to be either obedient or disobedient to the Word of God. And the only person we can and should be in control of is ourselves.

There are no pat answers or quick fixes for the battered woman. Many would disagree with that statement and say, *'Yes there is! Leave him!"* But battered and formerly battered women know differently.

The battered *Christian* woman, however, does have an edge, but only if she will submit herself wholly to the direction of God, commit herself to acknowledging him in all her ways, and allow *Him* to direct her paths.

My journey has not been an easy one. No woman's is who has had to deal with spousal abuse—and far too many women are still struggling with the awful fact of domestic violence in their lives. I feel I have traveled through a strange country that had never been mapped, yet there were so many who felt they could navigate me through it using *maps from **other** countries.*

I was trapped in a minefield that multitudes of women spend their entire lives trying to navigate and many never find their way out of. But with God's help, I found my way out. And I mapped my journey. It is my hope that other women might find my map helpful in successfully navigating their own minefield.

New Life

Testimony of the Author

*"I was finished with God, Jesus, Heaven, Hell, Christianity and anything that had to do with it. God truly found me at a time when I was **not** looking for him. . ."*

I was only six years old the day I decided I wanted to belong to Jesus Christ. I went home feeling a sense of euphoric joy. *A sense of joy that was not to last . . .*

I don't remember the sermon topic that day. Theology was not a concern at the time. I only knew that when the Pastor gave the invitation to "join the church," I wanted to. And as he counseled with me and prayed with me, my six-year-old faith connected with God through belief in his risen son, and I knew that something special had happened to me.

I would like to say I was faithful to God after that, but I wasn't always.

My Mother made sure we were at Church almost every Sunday, and I said my prayers at night sometimes, but I never made Jesus a real part of my life. I had no idea how to do that.

As an adolescent, I went my own way and stopped going to Church altogether.

A fear of dying and going to hell descended on me

and stayed there for the next eighteen years. The only thing I knew about being a Christian was that you were supposed to go to Church and live a certain way, and I didn't want to do that. To be perfectly honest, church bored me.

As a young adult, I began living a lifestyle that I could not reconcile with my conscience (and with what I had been taught in Church and in Sunday School throughout my childhood).

In 1979 the guilt and fear became almost unbearable, and I decided I did not want to believe in hell anymore.

The only logical way that I could accomplish that goal . . . was to stop believing in God.

I know it sounds ridiculous, but I was very serious about it. I reasoned with myself that if the scriptures were true and there was a God, then there surely was a hell, and in spite of my profession of faith at age six, I was certain I was going there.

I could not think of a single reason why I should be granted eternal life when I died. I did not understand that it was faith in what Christ did and not my own good works that would save me.

I will never forget the first time I announced to another person that I did not think I believed in God.

140

The words shocked us both. But lightning didn't strike, and I felt encouraged to pursue my goal of becoming an atheist.

Between 1979 and 1981 I worked very hard at it. Sometimes, during the day with all its distractions, I was somewhat successful. But at night, when the silence descended, I could not squelch the conviction of the Holy Spirit that the scriptures were true and that God was real.

In 1981 I was invited to go to church with some friends and family, and I went. I did not go to worship God that Sunday morning. My goal was to discount everything the preacher said and prove that Christianity was a myth—a crutch for weak-minded people to lean on.

I successfully (to my own satisfaction) shredded everything the preacher said that morning. I sat through the songs, prayers, preaching and altar call completely untouched emotionally or spiritually. I walked out of church unchanged and very satisfied with myself.

I went back again the next week. I knew that if I could sit through one more sermon and altar call unmoved, as before, that I would be free forever from this Christianity thing that tormented me so.

I planned on walking away from God that morning and never looking back.

I sat down on the very back pew, the one closest to the exit, and waited for the service to begin. The congregation stood up, said a few prayers, and sang a few hymns, then sat down.

I felt nothing—so far so good.

Then the preacher (who did not know me) raised his arm and pointed his finger directly at me and thundered the first words of his sermon . . .

"And God gave them up!"

When he uttered the last word of that sentence, something seemed to come out of the end of his finger and slam straight into my heart. In that moment, all of my atheistic defenses were shattered, and I became acutely aware of the existence of my God and Savior, Jesus Christ.

I immediately cried out to him in my heart. I told him I knew he was real, and I was sorry for ever denying him. I don't remember anything else the preacher said that morning, but I was the first one to reach the altar when he finished preaching.

I picked up my Bible that very afternoon and began reading the New Testament book of Matthew. I have been reading my Bible daily for over twenty-five years now. I read my Bible straight through, over and over, always picking up today where I left off yesterday. It has changed my life.

It took me almost twenty years to pick up where I left off when I was six, but I know that God allowed a little child to come to him, and then held on to her and mercifully revealed his awesome presence, even as she tried with all her might to deny him.

Bibliography

The Holy Bible, King James Version

Alsdurf, James, Phyllis, *Battered Into Submission*, Downers Grove, Illinois: InterVarsity Press, 1989

Cassell, Marianne, *Me, reverence my husband?*, Fort Worth, Texas: Harvest Press Incorporated, 1980

Dobson, James, *Love Must Be Tough*, Colorado Springs, Colorado: Multnomah Publishers, 1996

Dodds, Elreta, *Is God A Chauvinist?*, Detroit, Michigan: Press Toward The Mark Publications, 2002

Elliot, Elisabeth, *Let Me Be A Woman*, Wheaton, Illinoise: Tyndale House Publishers, 1982

Forward, Dr. Susan, Joan Torres, *Men Who Hate Women & The Women Who Love Them*, New York: New York, Bantam Books, 1986

Hagin, Kenneth, *The Woman Question*, Tulsa, Oklahoma: Manna Christian Outreach, 1975

Handford, Elizabeth Rice, *Me? Obey Him?*, Murphreesboro, Tennessee: Sword of the Lord Publishers, 1972

Norwood, Robin, *Women Who Love Too Much*,
New York, New York: Simon & Schuster Inc., 1985

Walker, Lenore, *The Battered Woman*, New York,
New York: Harper & Row, 1979

Associated Press. *China Facing Major Gender
Imbalance*. Beijing, China (January 12, 2007).

Suggested reading
(the links below may or may not be active)

http://www.fbi.gov/ucr/ucr.htm

http://www.fbi.gov/ucr/05cius/offenses/violent_crime/murder_homicide.html

http://www.fbi.gov/ucr/05cius/offenses/expanded_information/murder_homicide.html

http://www.fbi.gov/ucr/cius_04/offenses_reported/violent_crime/murder.html#table2_11

http://www.adherents.com/rel_USA.html#religions

http://www.turningpointinc.com/reports/2001-Turning-Point-AR.pdf

http://www.library.ca.gov/SITN/2003/0351.htm

http://www.ojp.usdoj.gov/ovc/publications/infores/clergy/welcome.html

http://archives.umc.org/umns/news_archive2003.asp?ptid=2&story=%7BE426D0E0-75F6-4FBC-96EE-2FF2401A0BCD%7D&mid=2406

http://www.methodist.org.uk/static/conf2005/co_domesticabuse_0805.doc

http://www.methodist.org.uk/index.cfm?fuseaction=information.content&cmid=336

http://www.biblebb.com/files/macqa/1301-N-13.htm

http://www.gty.org/resources.php?section=positions&aid=192

http://www.xyonline.net/misc/vstatsweb.html

http://www.eurowrc.org/06.contributions/1.contrib_en/27.contrib.en.htm

http://pollysplacenetwork.com/PDFs/Church.pdf

http://www.actabuse.com/whyshestays.html

http://www.soencouragement.org/domesticviolence.htm

http://www.aardvarc.org/dv/religion.shtml

http://www.ncadv.org/files/DV_Facts.pdf

http://www.mincavaasordered.umn.edu/documents/toledl/toledl.txt

http://www.svsu.edu/writingprogram/braun03/ls_domesticviolence.htm

http://www.opdv.state.ny.us/criminal_justice/corrections/bip/bipintro.html

http://www.mincava.umn.edu/documents/battererprogram/battererprogram.html#id2295179

http://www.mincava.umn.edu/documents/battererprogram/battererprogram.html

http://www.dvalianza.org/resor/sum_eval_interventions.htm

http://tigger.uic.edu/~lwbenn/lwb/vawnetbatterer.htm

http://www.iup.edu/maati/publications/15MonthSummary.shtm

http://www.treeofhope.com/prevention.htm

http://www.iup.edu/maati/publications/ExecutiveSummary.shtm

http://amendinc.org/answers.htm

http://www.iup.edu/maati/publications/CDCFinalReport.shtm

http://www.gazette.rcmp-grc.gc.ca/print.php?category_id=55&article_id=44&page_id=51&lang_id=1

http://www.wfn.org/2003/03/msg00184.html

http://www.gcumm.org/News/NACP%20Meeting%202003.htm

http://www.forensiceducation.com/sourcebooks/glossary/b.htm

http://www.forensiceducation.com

http://www.expertlaw.com/library/domestic_violence/battered_women.html

http://cyber.law.harvard.edu/vaw00/melner.html

http://home.cybergrrl.com/dv/stat/statgen.html

http://www.womensenews.org/article.cfm/dyn/aid/911

ABOUT The AUTHOR

Author and speaker Jocelyn Andersen lives in Central Florida with her husband Butch Watkins.

In addition to writing books, she publishes the online magazine, *"God's Amazing Love"* www.GodsAmazingLove.net, and writes broadcast material and web content for their website, www.HungryHeartsMinistries.com and their online radio station www.ShareCropperRadio.com .

Jocelyn can be contacted by emailing:

jocelynandersen@tampabay.rr.com

or by writing:

P.O. Box 1954
Auburndale, FL 33823

Books By Jocelyn Andersen

Redemption: Bible Prophecy Simplified

The day The Towers fell was prophesied in the Bible.

The basket of currency connected with the Euro is found in the Bible.

Details concerning the Rapture, The Great Tribulation and the first 1000 years of Christ's reign on earth are looked at from the unique perspective of the seven prophetic feasts of the Lord found in the book of Exodus.

This Book presents us with a panoramic and chronological overview of God's plan of redemption for our souls, bodies and this earth as revealed in scripture.

This book is simple enough for beginning prophecy students, but there is plenty to intrigue the intermediate and advanced student as well. Daniel's 70 weeks are examined in detail and the symbolism in Zechariah chapters three and five is unlocked. The Bible clearly reveals the methods the antichrist will use in his rise to power and the location of his home base.

When God's Great Redemption is Understood, Bible Prophecy is No Longer Complicated or Mysterious

125 Years of Bible Version Debate: Why?

Which versions Are trustworthy?

What is the real issue behind the Bible version controversy?

Are you armed with the basic facts?

It truly does go deeper than simply debating about which version is best. Jocelyn Andersen gives a simple treatment to a subject that has been unnecessarily complicated for far too long.

With 200+ versions to choose from, this book empowers the average reader to make an informed decision when choosing a Bible.

My Denomination Does Not Promote
New Age Spirituality
Through
Spiritual Formation!

There are two movements advancing at lightning speed through the Body of Christ today.

Both movements promote a spirituality which corrupt believers from the simplicity found in Christ by weaving New Age/Occult precepts and practices into the very fabric of their lives and faith.

This is done in such subtle and seductive ways that a complete paradigm shift begins to take place. Once this happens, the believer is completely unaware that the process of becoming prodigal has begun.

The Word of God becomes secondary to the experiential, and the danger of becoming apostate, at that point, becomes a real possibility.

LaVergne, TN USA
03 February 2010
171983LV00005B/73/A